MAN UP!

40 devotions for Christian men
who want to finally act like it

By Tim Baker

ISBN: **0615513581**
ISBN-13: **978-0615513584 (Tim Baker)**

DEDICATION

To my beautiful wife Amy.

INTRODUCTION

It's time to man up!

I don't know what has happened to men – especially Christian men – since the time that Jesus walked on this earth – but we have become wimps. It's time for us as Christians to reclaim what went wrong so many years ago.

We aren't the leaders of our families. We aren't taking charge of our spiritual lives. We aren't doing bold things for Jesus. We aren't defending our faith. We aren't preaching like this really is a life or death issue. We aren't doing anything that Christianity was built on.

We need to start acting like men again. Like the warriors of old in the Bible who would fight and die for what they believe in; who would follow God no matter what the cost. It's time to stop being wimps and time to start living our faith on our sleeves.

This devotion book is for 40 days. Why? It seemed like the right number to me. The floodwaters rained down on earth for 40 days and 40 nights. Jesus fasted in the desert for 40 days and 40 nights. Most habits take about 5-6 weeks to form – and 40 days is 5 weeks and 5 days.

Here's the deal. Each day you have verses to read, a little synopsis of what's going on in these verses, and some questions to answer. Here's the deal. I'll give you the verse reference but you need to look it up yourself. Real men read their Bible – not the Bible reprinted on the page. So pick up your Bible and read it. Don't have one? Borrow one from the library, purchase one, ask your church for one or write me and I'll be happy to send one to you. Don't make excuses, and don't just skip over the verses thinking you can get everything out of this without reading them. You're missing out on what God wants you to hear – the words He gave specifically for you.

Each devo has questions at the end of it for you to reflect on. All I ask is that you are honest with yourself and with the answers you give. Anyone can write Sunday School answers and fake it. But this isn't about being fake – it's about being real. No one's looking over your shoulder or will read them, so just answer honestly and truthfully.

Each day will also have what I call a "Man Up Challenge." This challenge is there to stretch you and to make you into a strong man for Christ. Don't just read the words and say, "Hey, this is a good idea." It's something to put into practice. Actions speak louder than words, so let your actions lead the way, man up, and do it.

Take this time to reevaluate what you are doing in your life and how you can improve it. Take this time to figure out where you are falling short and where you need to step up. Take the challenge. It won't be easy, but you'll be a stronger man at the end if you do!

It's time to man up!!

Day 1: Choose Your King

Verses to Read: Joshua 24:1-15

It all comes down to a choice. Who is in charge for your life? You or your God?

Joshua knew the answer to that question. He had been leading the Israelites through their military campaign and they had finally accomplished everything God had them set out to do. And so now was the time for them to depart as being one large group, and live with their own families as one nation.

Joshua told them God was the one who brought them there, who accomplished everything for them, who saved them from the hands of slavery in Egypt – and now they had a choice. They could go back and worship the Egyptian gods, or even take some of the gods of the land as their own, or they could choose the One True God who had been there from the start. Joshua knew who he was going to choose. For him, it wasn't even a question.

And yet, here we are many years later. In our world, gods don't exist in the same way they did back then, but we do have plenty of idols that we worship: TV, computers, the next big electronic device, cell phones, pornography, alcohol, drugs, greed, fame, power, fill-in-the-blank here. They are all things that pull us away from our worship of our One True God. They are the gods of the land we live in. What we are told we are meant to worship, to strive after, and to attain. But it is not what God has asked of you.

The question I have is: Are you ready to choose? I know some of you would say, "I already made up my mind. I've been a Christian for years now." But you can say you're a Christian, and let it just be a mental choice. Something you say you did. Something you said because you rationalized to yourself, "Forever in heaven is so much better than forever in hell, so I might as well make sure I get to heaven by saying I believe." Choosing between following God or not is not a matter of getting a ticket punched to heaven.

Making that decision to follow Jesus is first making the decision and then it is something you live out. This is a call for something more. This is a call for something bigger. This is a call for deep, gut-wrenching, Christianity. This is taking your mental decision and making it a heart decision. This is about making the word "Christian" less of an adjective, and more of a verb.

It's time. Three words - "Choose your King." There are enough Christian posers out there in the world already. We don't need anymore people who put on their Christian self on Sundays just to neglect it the rest of the week. You can't serve the gods of this world and the God of the World. It's one or the other.

God is looking for true obedience. God is looking for true 24 hours a day, 7 days a week faith. God is looking for people to cross the line from "I'm the king" to "I'm not worthy." From "I'm going to do what I want when I want how I want" to "Lord, let your will be done. Use me as you see fit."

This line is made of fire. I'm not going to lie or sugar-coat it. If you cross it, you will get burned. It will hurt. It's not an easy thing to do. But if you walk through it, if you come out the other side, you can finally be ready to take your faith to the next level.

Are you ready to put your faith into action, become on fire for Jesus, and get burned? The pain may be temporary, but the benefits are eternal.

Questions

1. What do you consider the "gods" of this world? What have people and the media told you about these "gods"?

    Money, Power, Materialism, Sex, Me, etc.

    They bring Satisfaction, happiness,

2. Why did you make the decision to follow Jesus? Is it a decision to continue to make every day?

    Because I was not fulfilled with the "gods" of this world. I was empty. It is a decision that I need to remake and choose every day.

3. How have you acted like a poser Christian? What do you need to work on?

    Just going through the motions. Not walking deeply/closely with the Lord. I need to give up control and submit my life to the Lord again

4. Do you think that making this decision will hurt? Why/ Why not?

It can hurt but would be more rewarding than continuing to just skate by. It would force me to trust/ depend on the Lord.

5. Do you think this decision is worth it?

Absolutely! I just need to get over myself and come humbly to the Lord.

Man Up Challenge

I want you to make the decision to follow God every morning. Every morning when you wake up from your good night's sleep, the first thing you need to see is Joshua 24:14. Place it somewhere you can't avoid it, and then pray each morning for God to be the king of your life. It's not a one-time decision, it's a daily one. Make it again and again.

Day 2: Which Path?

Verses to Read: Jeremiah 6:16-20

One thing I love doing is playing role playing games or RPGs. I don't know what it is about the game, but there's something about it I just get sucked into. Maybe it's the story line, wanting to know what's going to happen next, maybe I wish I was this guy wielding a sword, going after bad guys, cutting them down before they could get to me, or maybe it's just a way to escape reality for a little while.

Well in these games, you always get to the point where you have to make a choice. You see the game makers aren't going to tell you which way is right, so you have to make a decision. It's part of the thrill of the game. Sometimes you guess right, other times you guess wrong. But there is a way around it. Most of these games have guides you can get explaining every secret in the game.

Here's the thing: Even if you have the guide, a special book someone creates to show you how to accomplish everything in the game, even if you have all the answers right in front of you, you still need to take a step of faith and make the choice to follow it. If you think the book has no clue what it's talking about and is attempting to trick you so you will lose, you're going to go right when it says to go left. It's as simple as that.

Well this is what happens in our faith too. God gave us The Answer. God told us where to go. He laid it all out for us in black and white. And unfortunately, in this passage, the Israelites were told what path to take to follow God and to be at peace with Him, and their response was: "We don't want to go that way." He tells them to listen for the sound of the trumpets, and the people respond, "We're not going to listen." So they were given the right path, they were given the answer, they had the guide, all they needed to do was follow – but instead they decided to not trust God and go in the opposite direction.

We need to follow Jesus because it is the only way that leads to the end of the level. If you want to go the other way, all you'll end up doing is backing yourself into a corner, having to fight your way out, getting yourself injured in the process – just like if you went the wrong way in a video game. You end up wasting your energy and much needed supplies to get back where you started.

So the question is, you're standing at the crossroads. Two paths – the right one and the wrong one. You have a choice in front of you. Which do you choose? Are you heading to the next level or is it game over?

Questions

1. Have you ever played a game when you ran in the wrong direction? What happened? Were you able to get out of it?

    _____

    _____

    _____

    _____

2. Have you ever had a reliable person give you advice and you completely ignored it? Did you end up following it after you tried the other way first?

    _____

    _____

    _____

    _____

3. Why do you think the Israelites chose not to follow
    the path God laid out for them?

    _____

    _____

    _____

    _____

4. Are you wasting energy trying to strive for something
    that is the complete opposite direction of where you
    need to go?

    _____

    _____

    _____

    _____

Man Up Challenge

To know which way to go, God gave you a guide to help
you figure out which path is right. However, most people
don't know what the guide has to say even though they
claim they believe and follow every word in it. So read
the Bible – start from wherever you want – at the
beginning, follow a reading plan, read a gospel,

whatever – but make sure you know what the guide says. Then follow it – go where it tells you to go and don't deviate thinking you know better. God has a 100% track record of being right; you have no reason to doubt Him.

Day 3: Me, Me, Me

Verses to Read: Deuteronomy 8:17-20

I'm sitting here trying to think of a way to begin this devo, and the first thing that comes to mind is "How do I want to write this?" Isn't that just the way we always seem to think? It is always what we want and how we want to do things, because, in the end, we want to be able to say our accomplishments are our own work, and nobody helped. Seriously, if someone helped, well that would just take away all your thunder and you would have to share the praise with someone else.

That is exactly the way this passage presents itself. God is giving us two things: a command and a warning. The command is quite simple: we are supposed to remember Him. This sounds like such an easy thing to do, but it's not. We are sinful people and thus we're full of all this pride, which causes us to want all the praise and glory for ourselves, leaving God in the dust. But to truly live for Him, we must do the total opposite. We have to give all the glory to Him. We don't really see it, but we're nothing without God. We wouldn't be able to do anything, because like verse 18 suggests, he gives us the "ability to produce wealth," and He can strip it from us too.

Seriously, right now, I may be the one putting words into my laptop, but they really aren't my words, they're God's flowing through me. I am just His vessel doing the work He commanded, and I've accomplished it through the power He granted me. I have no English background, I'm a science geek, and to go one step further, I may have finished seminary, but there's so much about God I don't understand fully. When God helps us in completing His will for us, we need to take the time to thank Him for what He has done.

The second part is the negative, or the warning God gives. He states if we don't worship and bow down to Him, we will be destroyed. Now, I'm not saying it in the sense that every time you do something and don't praise God for it, lightning will strike you dead. We have to think long-term here. If we never give props to the one who does it all, we act as if He doesn't exist, and therefore we forget all about Him. If we don't respect God, and don't follow His words in the Bible, it's almost as if we don't believe in Him or His Son. If this is the case, we will be destroyed. Maybe it won't be when we walk the earth, but when you're facing that judgment seat of God, and you don't know Him, and you never praised

Him, He won't know you. And if He doesn't know you, you'll be cast out into hell, and there will the destruction come.

So when God accomplishes great things in your life, and you're able to do great things you never thought possible, just remember it is God who does it, and not you.

Questions

1. Before you start your day, do you ask God to be a part of it?

   Not Usually.

   _____

   _____

   _____

2. Have you ever caught yourself doing something, no matter how big or small, neglecting God in the process?

   All the time. I take much pride
   in what I do, forgetting that
   he gives me the strength and ability

3. When something good happens, whether it is at work, school, or wherever, do you give God the glory for it?

Sometimes,

4. Now if you do give God the glory for it, when others praise you for your actions, do you let them know it was all God?

Rarely.

Man Up Challenge

From now on, before you start your day, before you start a task, no matter how trivial – whether it is doing paperwork at your job, driving home after a long day, or watching your kids at a soccer game – take time to give God the glory for what is going on. Ask Him to be with you in the situation and to help you accomplish your task, or enjoy the time, or whatever it may be. It might seem weird at first, but the more you give the little things to God, the easier it is to constantly keep Him in the forefront of your mind.

Day 4: Spit You Out

Verses to Read: Revelation 3:15-16

These are some harsh words. These were words spoken to the church of Laodicea, a church which Christ called neither hot nor cold...but just...lukewarm.

So why is this just a great insult? Why does it attack their Christianity? What's wrong with being lukewarm? Where Laodicea is located, two rivers converge to create the water supply for the town. The problem is, one of these rivers came from Hierapolis, a place known for their hot springs, a useful tool for relaxation and restoration. The second water supply came from Colossae, a place known for their cold, refreshing water, which was useful for quenching thirst on a hot day. So when the water got to Laodicea...it was warm, full of mineral deposits, and just plain nasty. It tasted so bad, people would get nauseous from it. The water wasn't good for anything. It was completely and utterly useless.

That's why the illustration was used to talk about their Christianity. Their faith was worthless. They played the part, acted the role, shouted "Jesus is Lord," but it was only a "Sunday" thing to do. It's what was expected of them as Christians. The Word of God never sunk down deep and became an everyday type of thing. They were poser Christians. And thus, they were lukewarm. Lukewarm water is not useful, just like poser Christians are not useful to God.

God wants you to be hot or cold. Doesn't matter which you are. People misread these verses all the time. Some read it as God saying He would rather you be "hot" for Him or "cold" against Him. But in these verses, being cold is a good thing. Being hot or cold means you have a purpose, you have a reason, you have worth in bringing about the kingdom of God. But if you are playing the middle, and being lukewarm – what you're really saying to Him is, "I really don't want to go to hell, so I want your salvation, but I don't want you."

God doesn't call us to be the "Sunday" Christian. God doesn't call us to be poser Christians. God doesn't call us to be the person who raises their hands and sings with all their heart at worship, and then doesn't follow what they learn the rest of the week. God doesn't call us to be lukewarm people. All He'll do is spit them right out of His mouth. Just as you don't like drinking nasty warm water when you're hot and sweaty...don't offer God the same in your Christianity.

One more thought, if God says He will spit you out of His mouth, what makes you think you are accepted into His kingdom? If you're spit out, you are rejected. If you've taken the steps to salvation and your life hasn't changed, you're being lukewarm. If God hasn't transformed your heart, can you really say you truly believed in the first place?

Questions

1. What does being a lukewarm Christian mean to you?

_____

_____

_____

_____

2. What aspects of your faith are lukewarm?

_____

_____

_____

_____

3. Are you a "Sunday-only" Christian? What do you do during the week prove that you aren't?

_____

_____

_____

_____

4. Do you listen to the sermon on Sunday and it has no impact in your life? Why/Why not?

_____

_____

_____

_____

Man Up Challenge

This is a real simple challenge. You go to church every Sunday, so now make it count. When you go to church, take notes, jot down something new you learned, or what you need to do in your life to make your faith stronger. Once you do that, put it into action. Most people miss that last step. It is one thing to know how Christians should live; it's a completely different thing to act like it day in and day out.

Day 5: Search Me O God

Verses to read: Psalm 139:23-24

How many of you men pray every day? It seems like a simple question, and I know most would probably say prayer is a part of your normal life. If it is not, then it needs to become one. Prayer is our time to talk to God – to let Him know what is going on in our lives. Even though He knows it all, He wants that relationship time with us. Just as you would talk about your day with your wife, He wants you to tell your day to Him too. So please start praying. It will be a huge blessing if you do. But there is one piece of prayer I want you to consider when you start.

The real question I want to ask is, how much is admitting your sins part of your prayer life?

If you think about it, it's a tough thing to do. It's a humbling thing to do. It's a time where we have to go before our Maker, admit all of our faults, and let Him know that we continue to be broken human beings. In essence, we must go to Him and tell Him we are failures. It's a "put yourself in a vulnerable state" thing to do.

At times, we may have the mindset that when we do something wrong, we feel guilty about it, say to ourselves we won't do it again, and move on. Just because God knows all and knows we're sorry, doesn't mean we've brought our sins before Him. Nothing can be further from the truth.

It's easy to pray when we want something. "I want more money to pay the bills God," "I want you to heal this person who is hurting God," "I want the cancer to be removed from my body, God." That is simple to pray because we are in need. We are crying out to our Master to be with us in our tough times.

But when we have to own up to our mistakes it's a tougher thing to do - even when we should have the same attitude. We need to eradicate sin from our lives. We need to get rid of it all and place it on the cross. And yet when it comes to admitting our failures and needing forgiveness – it is sometimes the last thing we will ask for.

Put yourself in a position where you have to walk up to your mom and admit you broke her favorite vase. Or how about walking up to your teacher and admit you cheated on a test. Or how about walking up to a friend and telling them you blurted their secret to everyone. So when it's time to face God with what we've done, it's just something you'd rather not do. It's hard because you're at the mercy of the person you're asking forgiveness from.

But just because we're already forgiven, doesn't mean we don't have to lay down our sins. To get forgiveness, we need to be willing to ask for it. So the next time you pray, I want you to read this verse. Focus on it. Meditate on it. Use this verse as a prayer to God for things you have done in which you have never asked forgiveness for. I know it's tough. I know you don't want to do it. I know you've probably done some things which you rather forget happened. But it's only when we humble ourselves, bring ourselves down low, can we really build a stronger relationship with God.

Questions

1. Do you pray on a regular basis? Why/Why not?

_____

_____

_____

_____

2. Do you find it easy to ask forgiveness for your sins, or do you try to avoid the subject?

_____

_____

_____

_____

3. Are you scared of reliving mistakes from your past? What would stop you from praying this prayer?

_____

_____

_____

_____

4. Do you know that God will forgive all your sins, no matter how horrible you think they are?

_____

_____

_____

_____

Man Up Challenge

I think we can all find someone in our life that we hurt and never asked forgiveness. For this challenge, I want you to contact that person and ask for forgiveness. It may have been a foolish fight from 20 years ago, but it is something that needs to be placed at the foot of the cross. I know this is a challenge, and may be extremely difficult to do, but as Christians, we can't let grudges fester, and so let's drop them and seek forgiveness where necessary.

Day 6: Battle Cry!

Verses to Read: Romans 13:11-14

This verse is a wake up call for everyone out there who calls themselves a Christian. Will the real Christians please wake up? This verse is a calling to all Christians to step up in their faith and let it mean more than just something you say you practice, something you say you do every Sunday morning for a measly hour, or something you say is a piece, just a tiny little insignificant piece of who you are.

We need a wake up call as Christians. We need to step up and do the job we were meant to do. We let all these problems get in the way of serving God. We let our schedule make us too busy, so God cannot get a single meaningful minute of our time. We let our past make us seem like we're too defiled, and God would never want anything to do with us because we are just too broken for Him. We let what we want to do make us too distracted, because hanging out with our friends for four hours instead of three is so much more important than taking even five minutes to pick up our Bibles and read it.

Why is it important for us to do so? Because Christ is coming back. Sooner than we think. Paul said it himself, the night is almost over. It's dawn and there are so many people out there who know nothing about Christ, or probably never even heard who He is. It's sad but true – even in America, a place that used to be known as a Christian country has people who never had a meaningful conversation about Jesus – ever. And here we are, either afraid to do anything about it, think we do not know the words to say, or just would rather be doing our own thing rather than serving God with all we have.

So it's time. It's time to be all we can be in the Army of the Living God. No more excuses. It's amazing that we can find excuse after excuse to not serve God, the most important aspect of our lives, but we never have to make an excuse for the things we desire most. We clear our schedules for sports – whether we want to play them or watch them. We clear our schedules for schoolwork. We clear our schedule for our friends. We clear our schedules for our jobs. But when it comes to clearing up our schedules for God, there's just always something that gets in the way and makes us not want to serve Him.

So who's ready to serve God with all your heart? The armor of light is here waiting for you...waiting for you to pick it up and put it on. To serve God with reckless abandon, to serve Him the way we need to be serving Him in these dark times, let's grab our gear and go to war.

Questions

1. With your faith, can you say you have been sleeping behind the wheel – doing the bare minimum?

   _____

   _____

   _____

   _____

2. Have you ever scheduled anything that conflicted with something that was there to grow your faith?

   _____

   _____

   _____

   _____

3. Have you ever rescheduled or even dropped something from your schedule so you can grow in your faith?

_____

_____

_____

_____

4. Based on questions 2 and 3, which of these questions is more likely to happen in your own life?

_____

_____

_____

_____

5. What can you do to make God a higher priority in your life?

_____

_____

_____

_____

Man Up Challenge

I want you to map out your average week. Grab a
planner, grab a whiteboard, go on Google Calendar,
make your own on your computer – whatever you need
to do to map out a whole entire week in your life. You
have 168 hours in a given week. I want you to block out
your regular activities – what you would normally do –
your job, travel time, school, homework, family time,
friend time – you get the idea. Place down every
possible thing you can think of. Now looking at the
fullness of your schedule, what can you give up to make
that Bible study meeting, that youth group meeting, to
just spend more time reading your Bible, or interacting
with fellow Christians. Your goal is to place in specific
times where God can be the primary focus, and then
follow it. Not say it's a noble thought – but take the
thought and make it an action.

Day 7: Work-a-holic

Verses to read: Ecclesiastes 2:17-26

We as men put a great deal of emphasis into our work. We are the providers of our families and so to make sure there is food on the table, we work. Some of our jobs are 40 hours a week, you're in, you're out, you're done. The next time you have to think about it is the next work day. Others have to work more, spending 10, 12, even 14 hours a day to make sure they get everything done.

Some of us stress over our job and the money we make. We see ourselves making so much money, but it is not enough to pay the bills or to provide everything we want in this world, and so we work harder, putting in longer hours and striving harder to gain that next golden ring. But the question becomes, when do we earn enough? When is it that we can stop, lay back, relax and say I make enough money so that I can take some time and focus on others things in my life?

The answer to that question is never. When we strive to earn enough – we never reach it. Look at Bill Gates at Microsoft or Steve Jobs at Apple – they have billions and billions of dollars, but is it enough? They keep working themselves to death trying to find that next new gadget, or new device that will revolutionize the world.

And the question we need to stop and ask ourselves is: Is it worth it? Is your job worth more than everything else in this world? Is your job worth more than your wife, your children, your family, your friends, your God?

Think about all the sacrifices you made for the sake of supporting your family. How many times did you miss out on spending time with your wife because you took work home with you? How many times did you miss your child's first steps, or first baseball game, or first dance recital, because that project needed to get finished? How many times did you not hang out with your friends because you needed to type up that report faster than was really necessary? How many times did you put off your devotions with God, because you needed those extra few moments to finish something at work, or get more sleep because you were exhausted?

In this passage, Solomon, who was considered the wealthiest king who ever lived, sat and pondered this thought of work. He called it meaningless. Because no matter how hard you work, and strive, and strain, and sacrifice to get ahead – at the end of your life, you will die and have to pass it over to someone who in one instant can destroy your legacy. And how right he was. After his reign, Solomon's kingdom was never the same, as it was split in two and each part ruled separately until they were both destroyed. Solomon did all the work to maintain the kingdom, only to have it destroyed later.

So find the things that matter most to you and hold onto them. Find time to love your wife and let her know you picked her for a reason and she is the most important person in the world to you. Find time to be with your kids and to show them that they deserve as much of your time as you can give them – that they are more important than your job or a TV show. Spend time with your friends, who will hold you accountable and keep you down the right path.

And most importantly, spend time with your God. The decision to follow Jesus is the most important one you will ever make in your entire life. All He desires is a relationship with you – but if He is not getting the time because everything else is getting in the way, then you're not living the way He has asked you to.

Questions

1. How much time and effort do you put in your work?

    _____

    _____

    _____

    _____

2. In your list of priorities that you are living by right now, where would you list work? Your wife? Your children? Your friends? God? TV? Movies? Make a list of them in order of most to least importance.

    _____

    _____

    _____

    _____

3. Now, based on what you read, take that list and arrange them where you honestly think they should be.

    _____

    _____

    _____

4. Are you willing to live from now on from the second list rather than the first? Why/Why not?

_____

_____

_____

_____

5. What steps can you take to make sure this list becomes more than just words on a page?

_____

_____

_____

_____

Man Up Challenge

Get yourself an accountability partner – another man who will partner with you and keep you on the right path towards Christ. Someone who will let you know if you get your priorities off-line with what you placed on this page. This isn't a one-time thing, but someone you meet with regularly to share your problems, your concerns, and your negative times, as well as the joyful ones. So find that person. There are plenty of men at your church who could benefit from the relationship you form too.

Day 8: Identified in Christ

Verses to Read: 2 Corinthians 5:16-21

If you were writing someone for the very first time, and you had to describe yourself, what would you say? Would you tell them about what you look like? Would you tell them how old you are, what grade and what school you go to / where you work if school is far in the rearview mirror? Would you tell them what you like to do for fun? Would you tell them if you're a male, female, or other? How would you answer that question?

Now the deeper question – would the fact that you're a Christian even make it into the letter? Did the thought of mentioning you are a Christian even cross your mind?

What is an ambassador? An ambassador is a diplomatic official of the highest rank, sent by one sovereign or state to another as its resident representative. Did you catch that? An ambassador is a representative, but is also one who is sent by the by the sovereignty it represents. We were sent by God, through His Son Jesus Christ to be representatives of the Kingdom of God into this world. We are the ones who show others who God is, by our own actions.

This passage speaks of being Christ's ambassadors, and to be an ambassador for something, we need to let people know what we represent. But how can we let others know we represent Christ, if we don't tell them in the first place?

And if we are unwilling to tell someone we represent Christ, how are we fulfilling our role as ambassador? Instead of being that light in the darkness, we are being cowards who want to stay in the dark. We are being ashamed of who we represent. That is not living our lives as a bold, courageous man...instead, it's living like a wimp.

Today I'm changing it up a little bit. I'm throwing down the man up challenge here - one that I'm asking you to do today. Not tomorrow, not when you feel like, not "when you're older" (never understood that one since you're 10 seconds older now than when you read the last sentence). You do it **TODAY!**

Be **Bold**! Let someone know you're a Christian and you represent Christ. It doesn't have to be some big production, just let someone who doesn't know you are a Christian know you are one. You can send them a card and let them know you prayed for them today. Let them know you're reading this book. Invite a friend to church, Sunday school, or youth group, men's group, Bible study, whatever. Even just be nice to someone and let them know you're doing something for them, because Christ did something amazing for you. Whatever it is...show yourself as a true ambassador for Christ.

You can't represent someone or something if you don't let people know who or what you follow. Don't hide your Christianity, but let it shine. Be the ambassador God is calling you to be.

Questions

1. Have you been acting as a true ambassador for Christ? Why/Why not?

Not to the full potential God wants me to. I haven't been walking closely with God so it has been difficult to portray him well.

2. Do you let everyone you meet know that you are a
   Christian? If no, what stops you?

   For the most part. Sometimes i get
   scored or the conversation doesn't lead
   that way.

3. What are some ways that you can tell someone you
   are a Christian that would work for you?

   Live it.

4. How can you be more bold in your decisions to tell
   others of Jesus?

   Through prayer and asking God for
   opportunities.

Man Up Challenge

Did you think the challenge was going to change down here? It's the same thing. **Be bold.** Go tell someone you are an ambassador for Jesus. Don't be a coward. Don't hold back. Do it today. No more excuses.

Day 9: Smashy, Smashy

Verses to Read: Isaiah 41:22-24

Is there something in your life blocking you from worshipping God? Is there something in your life that gets more praise than God, gets more attention than God, gets more of your focus than God? Is there something that isn't important but prevents you from spending time with Him on a regular basis?

God strictly told us not to worship idols. It was so important, God put it multiple times in the Bible. In today's world, idols aren't what they used to be. We don't really make any more idols of gold, silver, bronze, or wood. But there are still idols in our lives. We have TV, money, Internet, materialism....all these things are idols in our lives. They are things that take our attention away from God. We can't read the Bible, because we're too busy seeing who's going to win that b-ball game. We can't go to church, because we need to make money to get what we need, but also what we want. We can't pray, because we need to respond to all our friends' status updates on facebook. All this is....is idol worship.

So as God said to the Israelites, I will say to you - bring in your idols, tell them to step up. Tell them to speak of what really matters in life. Can TV really predict the future and let us know what's going to happen? When I watch the news, they can't even get the weather right...how would they do when it's something more worthwhile? Can earning money bring salvation? Last time I checked, you can't buy your way to heaven. I read an article today saying 793 billionaires own a total of $2.4 trillion. Even that much can't earn one of them salvation, so why give it the power as if it could? Is the Internet the way to salvation? Yeah you can find some great links pointing in the right directions...but the truth is...there are more people looking in the wrong places, finding acceptance in stuff that is no where near the perfect acceptance Christ can give.

So it's time...time to go idol smashing. If something is in your life that's dragging you away from God, it's time to cut it out. If TV is dragging you away from alone time with God, take it out of your room, ditch the remote, give it away. If working 3 jobs is keeping you away so you can plan big vacations or buy new toys, cut back on your expenses so you can give up a job and give God the time He deserves. Or if the Internet has you wasting hours on end or surfing to the wrong sites, disconnect the Internet at home, or get rid of the mouse so God can get the glory.

An idol is anything you make to be one. If it takes away from worshipping God, you need to get it out of your life. So pick up your "bat" and go "smash" those idols.

Questions

1. What has been a major obstacle between you and God?

_____

_____

_____

_____

2. Do you recognize the idols of our culture as idols, or something else?

_____

_____

_____

_____

3. Do you truly believe you cannot earn your salvation?

_____

_____

_____

_____

4. What are you willing to give up for God?

_____

_____

_____

_____

Man Up Challenge

It is smashing time. In the Old Testament, the difference between an okay king and a great king was that a great king would smash and burn every idol within the country's borders. You need to be a great Christian. So find the thing that is keeping you from living up to your full potential for Christ, and get rid of it. If it's the cable, cancel it. If it is the internet, have someone block the sites that cause you harm or get rid of the service. If it is your job, find ways to not let it rule your life. Whatever you need to do, start smashing the idols from your life. Your faith depends on it.

Day 10: To Sacrifice or Not to Sacrifice?

Verses to Read: Micah 6:6-8

God doesn't want sacrifices; He wants us to do what's good and right in His eyes.

Think about it for a second: we live in a different time than Micah, so we kind of lost the context of this verse over time.

Back in Israel, they would offer up an offering whenever they did something wrong. This offering was called a sin offering. I know, real original. This offering, usually a blemish-free lamb, goat, or oxen, would take the place of the person's sin, by having the animal's blood spilt in their place, thus removing the person's guilt, and allowing him to continue to be in the presence of God, and His chosen people.

We don't live in this world anymore. Why? Because we have Jesus. Jesus has already come. He was already here and was nailed to a cross for all our sins. He lived the perfect life, free from sin, as these animals were also free from blemishes, and Jesus was able to be the sacrifice for us. Now instead of throwing an animal onto an altar for sacrificing purposes, we can just cry out to God for forgiveness and be covered by the blood of Christ.

But this does not mean we have a free ride to do whatever we want in life. Just because Jesus' blood can and will cover all of our sin, no matter how bad they may be, it does not mean we can continue sinning.

For Israel, God didn't want animals sacrificed to Him when they did wrong. God didn't want to see calf after calf being thrown up on the altar. Although every calf worked as a substitute for their sin, it didn't mean He wanted a person to be constantly at the altar. For us, God doesn't want to see us on our knees begging for forgiveness either. He doesn't want to see us crying out for mercy over and over and over again for the same sins. Yes, He commanded both these things, but just doing this is missing the point.

God wants obedience over sacrifice. He wants you not to do it in the first place. He would rather see you follow His commands, than to have to come back humbled in guilt. He would rather see you living a life that was honoring to Him, rather than making mistakes and repenting of them repeatedly.

Is there any sin you have you're struggling with? Is there any sin that wins more times than it should? Give it to God, ask for help, read His word, and find someone you know and trust who can hold you accountable, someone who can come along side you to help cut this sin out of your life. Act the way that is honoring to God in the first place, and remove the necessity to repent.

Walk the walk of obedience, not the walk of constant sacrifices.

Questions

1. Since Jesus covers all your sins, do you think at times that you have a free pass?

   _____

   _____

   _____

   _____

2. Have you been committing the same sin repeatedly, and constantly going back to God to ask for forgiveness? What is that sin?

_____

_____

_____

_____

3. If you fail at stopping yourself from sinning, do you lose hope and feel like you might as well continue because it's "too late"?

_____

_____

_____

_____

4. What can you do to remove that sin from your life?

_____

_____

_____

_____

Man Up Challenge

Obedient living does not happen overnight. It is something that needs to be worked on over a period of time. But the best thing to do to stop yourself, is to get a symbol. Something you wear, something you put in your pocket, something you place on your desk at work, that helps remind you of this commitment to holy living. Find a symbol and start reminding yourself that a life of obedience is far greater than a life of asking for forgiveness.

Day 11: Plans for Life

Verses to Read: Jeremiah 29:11-14

These are some interesting verses. And honestly, I have read these verses time and time again, because these verses are special to me. I would call them my life verses. They are the verses I turn to when I need encouragement, to remind myself that God is still there, God has a plan, and God is going to execute that plan in my life.

But I want you to sit back and actually look at what the verses say. **God says** - "For I know the plans I have for you..." So here's the lob ball question: Who does the planning for your life: you or God? God is the one with the plans, so God is the one who does the planning. We always bog ourselves down with planning the next great thing or the next big event ourselves. But what we're doing is taking God out of the equation. We want God to bless our plans – the plans we make with our own hands, rather than fulfilling the plans God has for us.

Now let's take it a step further. God has the plans for us. He has the plans to prosper us. So what do we need to do? What is our role in all of this? It is God's job to plan and it is our job to get ready for what the plans will do in our lives. How do we get ready? We find out in verses 12 and 13. We need to pray. We need to seek God out. It is only when we truly seek Him do we find Him. And then we need to allow Him to reveal His plan to us, rather than jump the gun because we got too impatient.

The verse says we will find God when we seek Him with all our heart. Praying with doubts is not seeking God with all our heart. Praying not expecting God to move is not seeking God will all our hearts. Praying while distracted by TV, or tiredness, or your cell phone, or your friends, or anything else, is not seeking God with all our hearts. Sometimes God is just waiting for us to do what He asks of us. We need to show Him we're ready. We need to show Him we want His will in our lives. We need to tell Him we're ready to shed the doubts and fears, because His plans are the plans that will change lives.

And it is only when we have our whole heart striving for Him, we are ready to move mountains. Faith the size of a mustard seed can move mountains. A little mustard seed worth of faith. The tiniest seed known in

Jesus' time. Just 1 mm in diameter. Having that much faith would be enough to pick up a mountain and hurl it into the sea.

Believe in Christ, believe in His power, and run after Him with no hesitations, and trust me...there will be mountains flying everywhere. So one question remains: Are you ready for the plans God has for you? If you answer yes, start chasing and don't ever stop, don't ever hesitate, and don't ever look back.

Questions

1. What are the plans for your life?

   _____

   _____

   _____

   _____

2. Are these the plans you made, or are these God's plans?

   _____

   _____

   _____

3. If you say those plans were yours, do you know what God's plans are for you life?

    _____

    _____

    _____

    _____

4. What is stopping you from fulfilling these plans?

    _____

    _____

    _____

    _____

5. Do you think you have enough faith to move a mountain?

    _____

    _____

    _____

    _____

Man Up Challenge

God gave us all plans, and some of us know them and others don't. So if you don't know God's plan for your life, get on your knees and ask God to show it to you. If you do know, or when you get your answer, it is time to act. No more putting it off. No more making excuses. No more pretending like it is something that is impossible. Moving mountains is impossible but God says it is possible if you have the faith the size of a mustard seed. It's time to build your faith and realize that mountains can start flying, if we just dare to believe it is possible and dare to act.

Day 12: Show Yourself!

Verses to Read: Judges 6:36-40

Does God need to prove himself to you? Here God was literally speaking to Gideon...in an audible voice. I just want to stop that thought to say that we try to figure out if God is present or not without hearing a word and here Gideon needed God to prove His power...not just once but twice...after having God speak to Him audibly. He asked God to make the ground dry and the fleece wet, then the fleece dry and the ground wet, and still He was a little shaky about it all God wanted him to do.

But are we any different from Gideon? I mean, yes, God doesn't seem to speak to people audibly anymore. But we always have that mindset, "If God would just show Himself like He did to Gideon, I would believe like that!" But the truth is, God is revealing Himself to us all the time, we're just not looking in the right places.

We have to see the little things. After I graduated from college, the very next day I went on a mission trip to the small town of Jaicos in Brazil. We went there to build a new church building for the town – one that would literally be a shining light on the town's hill. The church a few months after leaving had some problems with mudslides, and needed to raise some money to rent a bulldozer and fix the situation. So they prayed for God to help them find a way.

Meanwhile back where I was living, on a whim, without even knowing the problems going on down there, I sent $40 down with some letters to help the church. I figured I had so much after experiencing how little they lived on each day that they could use this for something. The amount of money they needed to fix their problems came out to $40 exactly. If that wasn't God at work, I don't know what is. They had a need, prayed, and God answered.

Someone may chalk that up to luck or a coincidence, or think that maybe I'm not telling the whole truth and they somehow let me know of their need along the way, but all I can tell you is that it was God. I just had this desire to help out those who had so little, and I gave what I could to them so that they could continue to reach people in there little town where rape, premarital sex, alcohol, and drugs run rampant.

We think we need a miracle to believe. We think we need to either hear God with out ears or see God with our eyes for us to believe. But God is with us. He has always been with us. He is performing miracles every day. We're just not looking in the right places, or not giving Him the glory when everything works out so perfectly. The next time God answers a prayer in your life, give Him the glory He deserves. He's working, we just need to work harder to believe He's the one doing it.

Questions

1. Have you ever had a time where you doubted God's existence?

   _____

   _____

   _____

   _____

2. Have you ever had an experience where God came through and you realized only He could have put that together?

   _____

   _____

_____

_____

3. When God does something remarkable, do you or others around you try to play it off as dumb luck or coincidence?

    _____

    _____

    _____

    _____

4. Do you need God to do something tangible for you to take that next step of belief?

    _____

    _____

    _____

    _____

Man Up Challenge

All you need to do for this challenge is to keep an open mind and to watch for God's work out in the world. Sometimes we don't see God working out in the world because we assume He's not. And so, all His perfect handiwork is neglected as sheer coincidence. I want you to go out and to watch for God in all that you do. Jot down some of your needs and watch God answer your prayers. See God at work in everything around you.

Day 13: Cheek Turning

Verses to Read: Luke 6:27-36

This is one of those passages we all say we don't need to go over again because we've heard it a million times and we know what it means and what we need to do. And I think that's great. So I just have one problem. Because it is that common and we heard it a million times and we know what we need to do, why aren't we doing it? Why don't our actions match up with what we know to be right?

Think about it. How many of us, when we get hurt by someone, just let it go? I would say not many of us. In fact, I would put myself in that category as well. When people hurt us, we find ways to hurt them back, or think about all the possible ways we can exact revenge on them. When they do something stupid that benefits them and puts us out, the next opportunity we get, we put them out. We're a culture of revenge, of equal justice, pure and simple. And unfortunately, we're using the golden rule in the opposite direction.

How many of us when seeing someone grab something of ours, even if it was accidentally, jump across the room, if necessary, and snatch it back for ourselves? And looking at what this passage says, how many of us are offering them more than what they wanted? The passage talks about when you're giving away your shirt, to give away your coat as well, even though they never asked for it. How many of us when we're asked for a dollar, give away 5, just because we have it and we want to help? But again, we earned and bought our own stuff, so we're not going to let anyone take it away from us – even if they ask nicely.

How many of us give when we're asked? I know at times I'm asked for things that are not worth much of anything, but I have this mindset that it's my pen and you can go get your own. But the guilt sets in and I end up giving it away, and what happens? They finish using it and they walk off with it. Figures, right? I help them out, and they take advantage. But Jesus is saying we need to give and give freely, not expecting or demanding it back, even if it puts us out.

So as I said, these are verses we know. They were ground into our heads when we were younger. We're continually told to turn the other cheek when we feel used and abused. But knowing something with your head, and doing something are two completely different things. Just thinking about doing the right thing is not as good as actually doing it. So instead of just going the bare minimum for God, let's stretch ourselves farther because as we serve those in need, we honor and glorify our amazing God.

Questions

1. Do you turn the other cheek, or do you hold a grudge?

   _____

   _____

   _____

   _____

2. Tell about a time you held a grudge or got revenge? What happened and how did it make you feel afterwards?

   _____

   _____

   _____

   _____

3. Do you freely give away what you have, or do you try to find ways to say no nicely?

_____

_____

_____

_____

4. When you do give, do you give more than what was asked for?

_____

_____

_____

_____

Man Up Challenge

People will always do stupid things because we're human, and you will get hurt by someone in the near future. It's just a fact of life. It's time for you to turn the other cheek. It's time to not let it overwhelm your life. Instead of getting mad and going through the list of ways to get revenge – just let it go. If they took something from you, ask if they need anything else. We need to start understanding that loving others and being there from them is far more important than fighting over stuff.

Day 14: Good Gift

Verses to Read: Luke 11:11-13

I remember hearing a story about this verse I want to share with you. I would give it credit if I remember where and when I heard it, and who told it to me. I'm not taking credit for this story, I just think it's a powerful one to ponder.

There was a father who had a son graduating from college. The father and son both discussed that he would get his son a car when he graduated. They would often look at this specific car in the window of the local car dealer. The son wished nothing more than the day he would get to ride that car.

The day of the graduation arrived, and after the ceremony, the father called his son into his study. He said how he was very proud of his accomplishment, and proud of the decisions he made in life. He handed him a box and wished him congratulations, telling him it's the gift he has been waiting for and a gift he hopes he treasures forever.

The son, filled with excitement, shredded through the box, and found in it a Bible.

The son was shocked and upset by what he saw. He was expecting keys, but instead he got a book he wasn't expecting. The son, upset and hurt, yelled at his father about how he promised him something and let him down. Then stormed out of the house, never talking to his father again.

Years upon years passed. The son went on to be a successful businessman. He worked his way to the top of his company, had a great family, a supportive wife; but still, never talked to his father, despite all his father's attempts to reach him.

Then one day, he was told of his father's death, a quick, sudden, unexpected one. He made arrangements and went to his father's funeral. Afterwards, he took some time to go back to his old house, and eventually into his father's study, the place where he last had a conversation with his father.

He noticed out of the corner of his eye, the box he threw on the floor, and the Bible he discarded, placed perfectly on the corner of his father's desk. He went over to it, and began to cry, realizing what he has lost. As he held the Bible, he thumbed through the pages until he got to a page his father marked. The verse highlighted was Luke 11:13, "If you then, though you are evil, know how to give good gifts to your children, how much more will your Father in heaven give the Holy Spirit to those who ask him."

Not only did the son notice the highlighted verse, but the piece of paper marking it. It was the receipt to the car of his dreams, the car he desired so long ago, dated 20 years ago as paid in full.

So after reading this story, I just want you to think for a second about what is a "good" gift. We call what Jesus has done "good news" and a "free gift" but is it a gift we give as high priority as other worldly, materialistic possessions? This is the greatest gift of all, so are you willing enough to bless others with it?

Questions

1. Have you ever expected a gift from someone and got something different?

   _____

   _____

   _____

   _____

2. Did you ever get mad at someone for not getting you the right gift?

_____

_____

_____

_____

3. Have you ever been let down by someone?

_____

_____

_____

_____

4. Do you value God's Word as much as you value your material possessions?

_____

_____

_____

_____

Man Up Challenge

If you are a father, are you living up to the challenge of teaching your children about the Bible? Are you practicing it in such a way in your home that they understand its importance? If you are not a father yet, do you see the importance of bring a strong spiritual presence in your future family? It needs to start now. You need to show your family that time in the Word is essential and important. They're not going to learn it out in the world, so start being that force, that light to them in the sea of darkness.

Day 15: Offering Your Worst

Verses to Read: Malachi 1:6-14

Do we really offer God our best? Do we really give Him the best we have to offer? Do you go to sleep every night knowing that God is a high priority in your life? Or is He just an afterthought? Do we offer Him our leftovers...the residual...whatever we have left after putting other things first?

These verses talk about how the Israelites were defiling God. God asked them for their best, their first fruits, the cream of the crop from their harvest. He also asked for their choice cattle, the ones without blemish or defect, the pick of the litter. And what did they really offer Him? The runts of the litter. Their weakest animals. The ones who were blind and wouldn't survive anyway if they let them live. The ones who got hurt in a fall, or caught a crippling disease, and just would have been tossed on the side of the road. That is what they offered God. Not the best, but their worst. The animals or fruit they didn't want anymore.

The question that pops into my head is, "Is what the Israelites are doing here true sacrifice?" What is a sacrifice? It's the surrender or destruction of something prized or desirable. So it's giving up something that matters to you, something tough, something difficult. Something you would miss if it was gone. Something that would cause you pain to hand away.

But how hard is it to give up something that is of no value to you in the first place, as the Israelites were doing to God? It's not. And that's why God was upset. They're not sacrificing, so it means nothing. It's a worthless act because it causes no pain by offering it to God.

And yet it's what we do to God all the time. Everything else is more important. Everything else takes precedence, and God just gets our table scraps. Think about it, it's only when we're done doing what we want to do that we offer our remaining time to God, if there is any left. Most of the time, it is at the end of the day, in a half-asleep stupor, trying to keep awake long enough to get through those few verses. It's only when we finish spending money on all the things we want and need do we consider giving any back to Him. We offer God our table scraps, our leftovers. In other words, we ask Him to accept our lame, blind, diseased animals.

It's time for us to give God what God deserves. It's time for God to get our best, our first fruits again. You wouldn't go to a dinner party with a half-eaten cake, spoiled food, and flat soda, so let's not do it to the God who loves us so much. He sacrificed His Son for us, so why should we be unwilling to sacrifice back to Him?

Questions

1. Do you offer God the best of your time, your money, your effort?

    _____

    _____

    _____

    _____

2. When have you ever given God "the runt of your litter" – something of absolutely no value to you?

    _____

    _____

    _____

    _____

3. When is a time you truly made a sacrifice to God?

_____

_____

_____

_____

4. How can you rearrange your schedule to make more time for God?

_____

_____

_____

_____

Man Up Challenge

It's time to sacrifice something to God. You need to think of the most valuable thing you own. As I say most valuable, I don't necessarily mean worth the most, but the one thing you know you would be upset about if you didn't own it anymore. You need to give that thing away. It is your first fruit. The best of the best in your life. If you want to serve God with all your heart, soul, mind, and strength, it needs to go. Show God and others that He means the most to you by being willing to sacrifice what matters to you most in this world to Him.

Day 16: Actions and Words

Verses to Read: 1 Peter 3:13-17

We are called to have our hearts so in tuned to God that we need to be able to give a person an answer to the questions they have about Christ. We should be a student of God so that we can be His representatives here on this earth. But two things are usually wrong about the way we go about doing this.

First, we think we're never good enough to talk about our faith. We feel like the knowledge that we have can never be good enough. At times, we think we need an advanced degree in theology or some deep grounded knowledge through many years of studying the Bible. But that never happened in the past. Jesus sent out His disciples, and they didn't quite know fully who Jesus was, but they brought glory to God despite it all. We feel we need to be able to answer every single question with pinpoint accuracy, and our fear of being stumped, or saying something like, "I don't know" would be the end of the world. But this isn't the case. Yes, we need to put

God first. Yes, we need to grow in our faith in order to learn more answers to questions. But we don't need to know all of them before we begin letting others know we believe in Christ. In fact, it is impossible to know everything about God because we cannot fully comprehend who He is, so if we wait until we know everything, we'll be waiting for eternity.

Second, we forget that last piece of verse 15, the gentleness and respect part. We see the people standing outside with signs that say "God hates *fill this space with whatever group of people God is mad at.*" We try to bully and argue people into believing our point of view, and if they don't agree, we just bully and argue them some more until they give up.

Where's the love? Where's the gentleness? Where's the respect? We'll do better winning people over with our actions, by showing them Christ's love, than throwing Bibles at their head, saying, "I love you, now believe before I force you to!" We cannot debate about God, because people will not change their minds most times because of how well you can argue. People change their minds because we become God to them – sacrificing ourselves: our time, our money, our energy, to show them how much Jesus sacrificed for us. Our actions pave the way, along with our words.

Love is what's needed. Love is the key. We need to first have that love for God that sets Him apart in our hearts. Then we need to show love to everyone around us. I guess it's one of the reasons why Jesus called them the two greatest commandments. It's not only the way we need to live; it's also the way we need to share Christ with everyone around us.

Questions

1. Do you ever feel like you don't know enough about God to talk to others about Him?

_____

_____

_____

_____

2. How much knowledge do you think you need to have to take that step to let others know about Him?

_____

_____

_____

_____

3. Have you ever tried to debate someone into believing in Christ? How did that go?

_____

_____

_____

_____

4. Did you ever show Christ's love through your actions? How did that differ in the person's response to you?

_____

_____

_____

_____

Man Up Challenge

You do know enough about God to go out and make an impact. So you need to go out and make an impact. Be willing to help someone who is in need today, and when they asked why you were willing to help, just respond with the simple message of "I believe this is what Jesus would do if he was in this situation, so as a Christian, I felt like I needed to be here at this moment to help." Nothing fancy, no big long debate, just let your actions and your words meet.

Day 17: Past in the Past

Verses to Read: Philippians 3:7-14

Do you have a past that you're not proud of – that you're embarrassed about – one you wished no one would ever know about? Is there stuff in your life that now you look back on and wish never happened? I think we all have those moments, those thoughts, those decisions we made that we're not proud of. We wish we could just get rid of them, or redo it all over again.

But this verse is speaking of putting the past where it belongs: in the past. To leave it there and to walk away. There's nothing you can do about it. No matter how hard you tried, how hard you worked, how hard you prayed to God, your past will still be there. It's permanent. I know if Paul, the writer of this verse, could turn back the clock, he would as well. He went out and killed Christians. He killed believers of Jesus because he thought they were insulting God, blaspheming Him. He had what he thought was a holy motive, and yet there is

nothing he could do about it either. It was his past –
who he was.

But all he could say about this was, "That was
then, that was who I was, my old self before I was
radically transformed, and this is now. It doesn't matter
where I've been anymore. The true matter is where I'm
now going, not where I once was." Paul was chasing
after Jesus. He had a new life, a new calling. He was a
new creation. Sure, he could spend countless hours
thinking about how he killed and arrested so many
Christians. He could spend so many sleepless nights
crying out, praying constantly thinking God would never
forgive him for his actions. He could just be still in his
faith, unwilling to move and not grow because no matter
how hard he tried, his sin was so great that forgiveness
could never be reached. But he didn't. He moved. He
followed Christ's voice. He ran after Christ and never
stopped his whole life. Despite his past, he was willing
to do whatever it took to bring honor and glory to God.

So you're at a crossroads right now. There might
be stuff in your life you hate, stuff you wish you never
did, stuff that you wish you could blot out of your
memory. But you also have a decision to make. You can
have your own pity party thinking, "Woe is me,"
believing you're too defiled, too broken, and too sinful to
be a follower of God. Or you can get up, shake off the

dust, and start walking after Him. It might start with baby steps, but over time those little steps will become a walk, a jog, a run, and then a full-out sprint after Him. But it's your choice to make. My prayer is that you already have your running shoes on.

Questions

1. What are things you have done in your past that you are ashamed of?

_____

_____

_____

_____

2. Are you constantly trying to change your past or forget it?

_____

_____

_____

_____

3. Do you think you are too defiled to serve God?

_____

_____

_____

_____

4. Do you have an answer as you stand at the crossroads? Do you know in which direction you need to go?

_____

_____

_____

_____

Man Up Questions

We all have a past; we all have things we wish we can change. But the last thing we should be doing is sell ourselves short thinking we are not good enough. We are all not good enough for God, but grace comes into play that no matter how bad we get, God will always forgive us through the blood of His Son Jesus. So it's time to let go of your sin. Write down the sins you are ashamed of. Compile the most exhaustive you can. Then tear it up to shreds. God doesn't hold the sin over your head, so neither should you.

Day 18: Taming the Tongue

Verses to Read: James 3:3-5

Isn't it amazing when something small can cause something big to happen? Look at the examples James gave here. You put a small bit in a horses mouth, this small little piece of wood, and what happens, we pull it in a specific way, the horse will move left, move right, stop or go. A boat can be so massive, but if you just take a little tiny piece of metal, sometimes only a few inches long, and turn it one way or the other, it can steer the whole boat.

This all seems to make sense. But the other piece of it is, no matter how much the horse may try or even the boat could try (yes, I do know a boat is an inanimate object) to go in a different direction, it can't. It's just not possible. It doesn't have the ability. The bit will hurt the horse so much that it will finally understand it is not worth fighting, so it will not be able to sustain going in the direction opposite of where it is being led. The same can be said for the boat. Even if you want it to go east, if your rudder is pointed to the west, that's where you're going. It is impossible for it to be able to change courses without changing the positioning of the rudder.

Well the same goes for our tongue. It's a very small part of our body, but think about how much it can steer us in the wrong direction with our faith. You can use it to lie to someone and bring down someone else's reputation, you can use it to make fun of someone you hate, you can use it to insult someone who messed up a job they needed to complete. Whatever it may be, it doesn't matter. A tiny little thing. This small little piece of the body can damage a whole person. Something so small and seemingly insignificant can steer you in the wrong direction and make your words not match up with the faith you proclaim.

This is so true in the world we are living in now, with bullying running rampant. We say a statement like, "Sticks and stones may break my bones but words will never hurt me." But words do hurt. They can cause someone to get depressed, being insulted time and time again with little or no chance of seeing relief. Words have that power to destroy. Words have the power to tear down. Words have the power to cause serious problems.

Some people will try to say, "Well, every once in a while is not a big deal." But as you all know, one little spark can start a raging wildfire. It just takes one insult, one lie, one little rudder change to take you off-course. One discarded cigarette. One little pop of a camp fire. That's all it takes to get a fire going. So the next time you're about to speak, make sure you keep to your faith and be a fire extinguisher, rather than a fire starter.

Questions

1. Have you ever been in a situation where you wanted to go in a different direction from the way you're being lead?

_____

_____

_____

_____

2. Have you ever started a fire with your tongue – telling a little white lie, making fun of someone, any other way you could think of?

_____

_____

_____

_____

3. Have you ever seen someone being bullied or have
    you ever been bullied? How did it make you feel?

_____

_____

_____

_____

4. How can you instead use your tongue for good?

_____

_____

_____

_____

Man Up Challenge

Use your tongue for good. Yes it is easy for you to tear
someone down, tell a lie or whatever. But instead, I
want you to use your tongue for good. Give some a
compliment today. Tell someone what a great job they
are doing with their job. Whatever you can think of –

use your tongue for good. We use our tongue so much to do evil, we as Christians need to start using it to do some good instead. Find ways to start today.

Day 19: Own It

Verses to Read: 1 Peter 1:13-16

Do you ever get desires to do the wrong thing, even though you know you shouldn't be doing it? It's a tough question to ask, because I don't think many of us would want to admit that such things happen to us. But I know there are plenty of times where I just get a though of "Man, that person makes me so mad, I just want to deck him on the side of his head," or something like that. It's an evil desire, and something we shouldn't be doing.

Before moving on, I would like to do some defining. What is the difference between ignorance and stupidity? Ignorance is not knowing the rules. For example, if you didn't read the sign that said, "No diving into the pool" and you chose to dive into the pool, you were ignorant of the fact you shouldn't do that. However, if you saw the no diving sign and dove in anyways, that is called stupidity. You're taking your life into your own hands, even though you know you shouldn't be acting that way.

These verses were trying to get across that before you became a Christian, you were ignorant to the rules. You didn't really have a good sense of what right and wrong was, so you didn't realize that such feelings as wanting to hurt someone was wrong. But as you crossed that line into Christianity, things changed. You do know better now. The difference between right and wrong went from something hazy to something crystal clear. You do know what you should and shouldn't be doing. Plus you should be able to rise above it all.

God is holy. I think not many would argue with that statement. God is perfect and blameless and never does anything wrong. He sent His Son Jesus to live on the earth, and he showed us how to be holy in all our actions and deeds.

We might look at Jesus and say, "That's just too hard to do! We can't be like Him." And in some ways, you're right. To live perfectly is impossible. However, even though it's tough, it's what we need to be striving for. We don't need to be perfect but we need to have out heart in tune with God's, and be motivated to go that extra mile.

We need to be holy because God is holy. Whatever thoughts or problems or mindsets we had in the past that are wrong, need to stay right where we left them....in the past. You can't take the old way of living into the new. You're changed. You're a new creation. And because of that, we need to be holy, just as God is holy. It's a tall order, but one that our powerful God can help us do, and He is with us every step of the way.

Questions

1. Have you ever done anything ignorant of the rules that you needed to follow?

_____

_____

_____

_____

2. Have you ever done anything stupid, knowing the rules but unwilling to follow them?

_____

_____

_____

_____

3. Do you ever confuse being stupid and ignorant – or claim to be ignorant when you're really being stupid?

_____

_____

_____

_____

4. Have you ever tried to live your new life in Christ by doing the same things before you decided to follow Him?

_____

_____

_____

_____

Man Up Challenge

Your Man Up Challenge is to man up. When you do something stupid, or even if it was ignorant and you honestly had no clue you were doing anything wrong, own up to it. Be willing to admit that you made a mistake. One of the biggest problems we have as human beings is that we don't own up to our own shortcomings and want to find a scapegoat. As Christians, when we fail, we should admit it, and not try to look for a way out.

Day 20: Walk through the Thorns

Verses to Read: Ezekiel 2, Matthew 28:18-20

How much different would the world be if everyone who claimed to be a Christian just listened to this advice from God? This passage is God calling Ezekiel into the life of a prophet. He tells him to not be afraid of the people he's going to be sent to. Even though they rebel against God, come after him and try to injure him, beat him, or even take his life, or even if they might not care at all what Ezekiel has to say. Ezekiel had one job and one job only – despite all the costs to himself, he needed to preach God's Word to the people.

And then there's us. We're Christians living in a rebellious world, dominated by people who could care less about God. And yet God not only commanded us to tell others about Him, He expects us to. Check out Matthew 28:18-20 again. That phrase, "Therefore go…" is not really a command; it was written as an expected action. A better translation in English would be "As you go…" As you go and tell others about me. Not, I order you to go. But if you say you follow me, this is what I expect you to do.

And what do we do? We are the ones who are afraid. We are the ones who don't want to walk through the thorn bush to let someone know about what Jesus did on the cross. We don't want to come close to a scorpion because we're afraid they might snap their tail at us. We're afraid of how that person would react to us and what we have to say.

I want you to think for a second about the person who brought you to Christ, the one who made the biggest impact in your life. Where do you think you would be right now if that person didn't come along, that person didn't take the risk to walk through the thorns and scorpions to let you know about Jesus? I don't think you'd be where you are today, and I know some of you might not even want to think about it.

So my question is, are you walking through the thorns? You got a new life because someone was willing to do what God expected of us. So why are you holding yourself back from someone else? Why are you not willing to go and do likewise for someone else? You are expected to go. You don't have a spirit of fear, but a Spirit of Power inside of you. It's now the time to use it and complete the task God asks of you. The interesting part of this verse is Ezekiel was told to speak for God, and if He didn't, he would be just as rebellious as the ones he needed to help. So why do we feel we can rebel and get away with it, or blow it off as if it's not a big deal? Grab your band-aids people, because it's time to walk through the thorns and get scratched.

Questions

1. What is the difference between a command and an expectation?

   _____

   _____

   _____

   _____

2. How does knowing that Matthew 28 is written as an expectation, rather than a command, change your thinking about what we need to do as Christians?

   _____

   _____

   _____

   _____

3. What stops you from fulfilling your duty?

_____

_____

_____

_____

4. Do you think your unwillingness to talk to others about Christ is just as bad as those who outright rebel against Him?

_____

_____

_____

_____

Man Up Challenge

When God calls, it is time to act. Most people hear God telling them to do something radical each and every day, but what ends up happening is, they decide not to do it because it seems either too far out there, or they would get embarrassed it if doesn't work out perfectly. But here's the thing: your comfort has nothing to do with this. When you hear God speak, do it. Don't wait. Don't hold back. Don't know if you're hearing from God or not? Just pray each day to open your eyes to someone in need and how you can bring Christ into someone's life. When God gives you that tug, trust me, you will know it.

Day 21: Hypocrites

Verses to Read: Romans 14:10-18

I want to talk about being a bad example. If there's one thing that destroys Christianity the most, it is when a person says one thing, and does the complete opposite. I think we all know what it's called...it's being a hypocrite. That's why people always focus on the bad things Christians do. A pastor who preaches fidelity and the sanctity of marriage is caught in adultery. A friend in a class who tells everyone not to pick on people, but in private he's the first to make cracks at others. A person quotes Bible scriptures about loving everyone, but is out on the streets with a picket sign saying, "God hates you for what you're doing."

These are extreme examples, but if you do anything to cause a fellow believer in Christ to fall, you're not setting a good example. In the passage we have here, Paul is talking about food being sacrificed to idols. He sees the meat as having nothing wrong with it, because he understands that this meat is clean.

However, if new Christians see him eating it and question their faith because of his actions, then he is not acting out of love.

If you tell people not to steal and you go out and cheat on a test (for those who want to tell me stealing and cheating don't relate: it's stealing answers you didn't know), how does that show you're a Christian? If you tell everyone you need to keep yourself pure sexually, but you go around the locker room bragging about all the hookups you had over the past weekend, how is that being a good example?

We need to be strong examples for Christ. If there is something in our lives that would make others question if we are truly followers of Jesus, we need to ask why it's a part of us in the first place. It's interesting but people who don't get Christianity know the basics. We're supposed to love others, be modest, be nice to everyone, including our enemies, and serve those who need help. But if the example we're showing is anything less than this...are we really being a good example?

I want you to pray to God today, and see if there is anything in your life that is holding you back from being a great example for Him. You won't become the perfect example, because no matter how much we strive to be, we will always have setbacks, and we will always sin. But this is more about asking if there are any daily choices we make which are stopping us from following Christ - whether it's the clothes we wear, always insulting an enemy whenever you see them, or lying to friends. Let's be the example we need to be. Let's show people what true Christianity is all about. If we don't, don't be surprised if someone calls you out as a hypocrite.

Questions

1. How are some ways you have acted like a hypocrite when it comes to your faith?

   _____

   _____

   _____

   _____

2. Have you ever been called out as one? What happened?

   _____

   _____

   _____

3. Is there anything you do that may not be a sin, but will make someone question your Christianity because of it?

    _____

    _____

    _____

    _____

4. What are some ways you can be a powerful example?

    _____

    _____

    _____

    _____

Man Up Challenge

It's time for you to check your life and see if you have an action that may not necessarily be sin, but when others look at you, it causes them to stumble in their faith. Maybe you watch R rated movies with scenes that are not healthy to your faith. Maybe you make little sarcastic cracks about someone when they are not around. Whatever it maybe, if it is causing another to weaken their faith, it needs to be something that is fixed in your life. Ask God to reveal it to you and than find ways to eliminate it.

Day 22: Being Ashamed

Verses to Read: Romans 1:8-16

These verses are tough ones, because they say, "I am not ashamed of the gospel." It doesn't sound that bad, but then you think about it.

When you don't want to tell people that you're a Christian, that's being ashamed of being a Christian. When you don't want to help the kid who's being picked on, that's being ashamed of being a Christian. When your friends want you to do something you know is wrong, and you decide to do it anyway, that's being ashamed of being a Christian. We do it all the time, we get ashamed of God because we want acceptance. We crave it. We desire it. And honestly, most of us would do anything for it, even if it means rejecting the God we say we love and believe.

But we have to remember: a person's acceptance based on what he does isn't eternal. It doesn't last. We live a "What have you done for me lately?" culture. Growing up a Red Sox fan in Boston, this is the constant mindset there. I will be the first to admit that Boston fans can be the worst when it comes to this concept. We would have a player who may have single-handedly won us a game, a series, a world championship. But if he struggles the very next season, just 4-5 months later, and has a .200 batting average, we would throw him under the bus and run him out of town. He's not doing anything to our liking anymore, so what do we do? He loses our acceptance. We ask if we could trade him for a few baseball bats or a bucket of baseballs.

But God doesn't work the same way. God's acceptance isn't based on our actions. If it was, trust me, He would be running us out of town like Red Sox fans do to ball players they hate. There would be absolutely nothing about us that would make God look at our actions and say, "Yep. He's a keeper."

But God accepts you for who you are, warts and all. You don't have to do anything special to make Him love you more. You don't have to go out of your way to impress Him. All you have to do is just believe, have faith, and follow after Jesus. And once you got it, even if you make a mistake, stumble, or fall, there's nothing you can do to make you lose it. He will still love you, still accept you for who you are, even if you don't think you deserve it.

So let's be honest, what's more important to you? Acceptance that lasts into eternity, or acceptance that lasts until you just have to prove you deserve it again? I know my answer, and I'm chasing after Christ. Where does your acceptance come from? Where do you get your value from?

Questions

1. Are you ashamed of the Gospel? What about it makes you feel this way?

_____

_____

_____

_____

2. If you are ashamed, why did you make the decision to follow Jesus in the first place?

_____

_____

_____

_____

3. Have you ever done anything to try to impress
   someone? How long did it last?

   _____

   _____

   _____

   _____

4. How does it make you feel that you don't have to
   earn God's love?

   _____

   _____

   _____

   _____

5. How does it make you feel that God will accept you
   with all your mistakes?

   _____

   _____

   _____

   _____

Man Up Challenge

It's time to stop being ashamed and start being proud of who you are, and what you believe. At some point today, you are being challenged to put your faith above your acceptance. To do the right thing over the popular. Do something that may be risky or even damaging to your reputation, but it will be something not done to find acceptance by others around you, but would be done because it is biblical and the right thing to do.

Day 23: Constant Worrying

Verses to Read: Philippians 4:4-9

Be honest; how much do you worry about every little thing in your life? How much do you worry about the bills being paid on time? How much do you worry about being able to put food on the table so you and your family can eat? How much do you worry about getting your job done by the time it's due, rather than passing it in late? How many of you worry about others in your life that don't seem to be going in the right direction, and just spiraling downward out of control?

It's a common thing to worry, but we need to not let it cover our lives. We have a God who is there for us, who answers our every prayer, and wants to hear from us in our times of need. When we get anxious about something and not give it to God, what we're saying is, "I have more faith in myself to get through this than I do in God to help me through it." You may not think or feel that way, but that's what your lack of action is saying.

God is there for you. He wants to help, but He isn't a God who throws Himself into a situation you don't want Him in. He wants you to be willing to invite Him in and to take care of it His own way. He wants you to want Him to help – if that makes sense. He'll wait for you to come to Him and ask.

But when you ask, you need to do it with a thankful heart and an expectant heart. God is there to help you, but you know what it's like to help someone who is ungrateful for what you sacrificed, so why would you do that to God? We need to thank God, not just when we pray and ask, but when He does pull through and answers our prayers.

Not only that but you also need to pray knowing and expecting He will act. If you go to God and pray something like, "God, I feel like I'm talking to a wall and I know you're not going to listen to me anyways, but I was told I need to pray so here it goes – please help my brother through this time," it's not praying to the God of the universe with expectation of Him to act. You're doing it out of feeling forced, rather than actually wanting Him to come down and act.

When He's there for you, when you finally get your answer, all that will be left is peace. When there's nothing to worry about because God is in control and took up the situation into His hands, there's nothing left to be anxious about anymore. All you need to do is relax and have peace, and let God do what He does best, take control of the situation.

Questions

1. Would you consider yourself a worrier? Do you worry more times during the day than you place situations in God's hands?

_____

_____

_____

_____

2. Do you believe God is there to help you? Do you believe He answers your prayers?

_____

_____

_____

_____

3. Do you ever pray without a thankful heart? Do you ever pray not expecting Him to act?

_____

_____

_____

_____

4. If you really think about it, have you ever had a time where all of your needs were not met?

_____

_____

_____

_____

5. Do you think your worry can change anything, and cause your problems to magically disappear?

_____

_____

_____

_____

Man Up Challenge

It's time to let it go – everything. Stop worrying about every single detail of your life and start trusting in the God who is in control of the whole entire world. I want you to write down all of your worries that you have right now, and hand them all over to God in an expectant and thankful heart. Now watch God move. When God answers your prayers, write down the answer He gives, and over time, just marvel in the fact that they are all met.

Day 24: Anger

Verses to read: 1 Peter 2:11-25

I know everyone has a time in their life when someone got them mad. I mean really mad. Something that got under your skin, made your blood boil, made that vain in your neck swell so it looked like it was going to burst. We all remember those moments in our lives, and the fact that I am bring them up right now rushes all those emotions to the surface.

So the question is, what did you do about it? Did you launch into a hot-headed tirade against the person who hurt you, listing all the ways they offended you? Did you yell in their face, scream at the top of your lungs, or swear at them? Did you push them, punch them, or get into some sort of physical altercation? Or did you just give them a nasty look, or treated them like dirt every time you saw them afterwards?

Why do we do this? Why is this our reaction when someone causes us harm? It's simple really. It's easy to react negatively to a person who got you mad.

It's easy to do all the things I listed above, because being nice, kind, and turning the other cheek takes more effort. It's easier to hold a grudge or get revenge.

Let's face facts. It's hard to love someone who hates you back. It's hard to do something thankless for a person who has caused you nothing but grief. It is hard to care for someone or feel sorry for someone whom you think got what they deserved.

But take a page from the Book of Christ. Look at His reaction to a tough situation. It would have been easy for Him to retaliate against those who arrested Him. It would have been easy for Him to stand before Pilate, listing all the ways these accusers of his have committed sin in their lives. It would have been easy for Him to come down off that cross and utter the words – the words that would unleash millions of angels to exact revenge for all He has suffered, slashing His accusers down left and right. He could have threatened them to try to make them back down or be afraid. But instead, He just allowed God to pay them back for their actions, in His timing.

God is the one who judges and will pay people back for their actions. Revenge and justice, no matter how much it may seem to be the right thing to do when offended, is never the answer. It's not our place to judge. We're not the one who's going to hold the other accountable at the end of time, because we're all accountable to the same God. So what we need to do is simply love and let God do what God is meant to do.

Questions

1. What is a way someone has offended you?

    _____

    _____

    _____

    _____

2. What has been your relationship with that person since then?

    _____

    _____

    _____

    _____

3. What typically happens when you get hurt by someone?

    _____

_____

_____

_____

4. How hard will it be for you to turn the other cheek?

_____

_____

_____

_____

Man Up Challenge

This may be a tough one for some of you, but it's something that is very important. When you are placed in a situation where you are offended, your goal is to not get angry. It sounds simple enough but it's not as easy as it looks. Our immediate reaction is to get red in the face and defend ourselves – the whole "fight or flight" response kicks into overdrive. But instead of unleashing your fury on this unsuspecting person, be willing and able to look past the offense, and to show love to that person, explaining calmly how they hurt you, and let cooler heads prevail.

Day 25: A House Divided

Verses to Read: Matthew 12:22-32

I think this is a great question Jesus asks in this passage. How can a divided kingdom survive when you're fighting most battles against yourself than your enemy? It's a question that most of us fail to answer. Why? Because we think it's a pointless question in the first place. What type of group would honestly fight amongst themselves causing conflict, stress, wasted energy, and eventually the ruin of everything they worked hardest for?

What would happen if a hockey team started throwing pucks into their own net rather than the opposing teams? They would lose. What would happen if a revolution to take over a country bickered over who should lead them, or become president after they succeed? They would fail, and possibly end up dead for treason. What would happen if a company thought their product should be produced two separate ways? They would have a higher cost, more waste, and go bankrupt.

It's just a fact, you don't fight amongst yourselves. It's a no-win situation and it's the biggest no-brainer.

But then you check out your own personal faith, and the church. And what happens? Constant fighting over everything. Old fighting young over the way it used to be verses the way it should evolve. Contemporary versus traditional over the great hymns of old and the praise music of this generation. Constant fighting, causing constant splits, causing a divided kingdom. Isn't it sad there are thousands of denominations in the world that all claim to be chasing after Jesus Christ? This is a problem people. A serious one too. How can we win people over, let them know the love of Christ, if our actions towards each other are not backing it up? If we can't get on the same page and start moving forward, we're just going to remain a broken kingdom – letting our thoughts and preferences override the love we are supposed to have for one another.

Let's step up. Let's fight the good fight the right way – against the enemy and not against ourselves. Let's realize that we can all worship God in different ways. Yeah, some like hymns sung a capella or with a piano and others like bands leading songs more upbeat, but who cares? As long as we're achieving the same goals of helping people find Christ, isn't that fulfilling our purpose? Isn't that leading people together in unity, rather than beating each other up? So let's help each other, rather than fight. Otherwise, we're just left with a broken kingdom, and as Jesus says, how can it stand if everyone is destroying it from the inside out?

Questions

1. Have you ever experienced fighting amongst a group of people? What happened? Why did it start? Were you able to solve the problem?

   _____

   _____

   _____

   _____

2. Do you go to a church where there is this type of in-fighting – people fighting against each other, creating an atmosphere of anger and frustration?

   _____

   _____

   _____

   _____

3. Are you willing to let go of your traditions and your preferences if it means bringing healing and peace back to your church?

_____

_____

_____

_____

Man Up Challenge

A divided kingdom will fall, so we need to be the ones trying to bring unity back to the church. When you get into an argument or disagreement with a member of a group you are a part of, remember this verse and try to bring peace back into the situation. Explain to each other that the group will fail if everyone is not on the same page, and a solution needs to be found where everyone is happy. It's not worth getting in the middle of the fight to continue the flames of hate – so be the one who is willing to get a pail of water to snuff the flames out.

Day 26: Calling out in Truth

Verses to Read: Psalm 145:13b-20

Don't you hate things that have fine print on it? "You won a free iPod! Click here to redeem." But it's not as simple as clicking on the link. You also have to put in all your personal information, which might end up being stolen or given away to some company to send you tons and tons of spam mail, complete two surveys about your opinion of burnt toast and spray cheese, sign up for a free credit report, which actually costs you $29.95 a month over the next year in identity fraud services, and then sign up for Netflix for $14.95 a month for the next year as well. Then after all this you get your "free iPod." So pretty much, this iPod that was free, just cost you $44.90 a month for the next year. Nice little trick they pulled.

But the good thing is, God isn't like that. God doesn't like fine print. God chooses not to use it. He'll just tell you what you need to know, when you need to know it. And what He says, that's what He'll do. You don't have to wait for the catch. You don't need to sign up for anything. You just have to trust Him. God tells the

100% truth every time so you know what He has to say is reliable and trustworthy.

So as we come to today's verse on prayer, we see that it was laid out specifically what we need to do to be near to God. All we need to do is simply called on Him. Now instead of putting it in a side note, instead of putting fine print, instead of sticking it on a long "Terms of Service" form no one has the proper magnifying glass to read, He lays out the next point in the same exact verse. God will come near to you if you call on Him in truth. There are no gimmicks here, no special circumstances, no tests to pass, no nothing. If you want peace with God, if you want to have a relationship with Him, all you need to do is call on His name in an honest, truthful manner.

You have to be truthful about calling on Him. If you call on Him asking for something in a selfish manner, you're not calling in truth. If you're calling on Him expecting Him not to answer, then you're not calling in truth. If you call on Him and really don't mean it, then you're not calling in truth. If you call on Him and don't really want Him to answer, then you're not calling in truth. If you want God's help, you need to mean it, believe it, and want it. Anything short of that, all you're doing is sending up a fake call to God. God can see right through you to your heart. If you're not willing to call

Him the right way, don't be mad if He doesn't come near.

Questions

1. Have you even been scammed by something that seemed too good to be true? What happened? Did you get what you were hoping for, or did it end up costing you more or being of lesser quality?

   _____

   _____

   _____

   _____

2. Do you believe God has given you all the instructions necessary to live your life for Him?

   _____

   _____

   _____

   _____

3. Are you truthful when you call on the Lord? Do you ever pray thinking He won't answer? Do you pray thinking He won't give you the right answer?

_____

_____

_____

_____

Man Up Challenge

Pray with conviction and pray in truth. Believe that there is no catch when it comes to God. Believe that when He says that all you need to do is come and ask Him in truth that He will deliver. Challenge yourself to believe what you are praying to Him, instead of thinking this is a pointless practice or that you're praying to a wall. Believe in the power of the God behind the prayer, and pray as if you know with your whole entire heart that he will come through and answer it for you.

Day 27: Do the Crime, Pay the Time.

Verses to Read: 2 Samuel 24

Don't you hate when you need to make a tough decision in your life, especially one that will affect the lives of everyone around you? If you make the right choice, things will go well with you, but if you made a bad one, it will cause everyone to suffer. That was the place David was in.

David committed a sin. David made the mistake. David counted his fighting men. Why is that such a mistake? Why did God get upset about this? By counting his fighting men, it showed that David placed more faith in numbers, put more faith in statistics than God. So what was the punishment? It was laid out for him in this verse. He had to choose between 3 years of famine, 3 months of being routed by his enemies, or 3 days of an epidemic.

I have to ask, if you were the king of the land, and God gave you this choice as punishment, what would you do? Most I asked said they would choose the 3 days of plague, because it's the shortest one, and it seems the least threatening. Most don't like losing, and the thought and fear of knowing that your enemies will constantly be chasing you and you will never be able to overcome them is very threatening. And I can tell you that I am a fan of food, so to think seeing my own people suffering and dying from hunger is not fun either.

But the point is, your choices have consequences. You can't make a single choice in this life and think there are no consequences for your actions. Here was a sin that David committed, and because of it and his choice of punishment (he chose the 3 days of disease), 70,000 Israelites died. 70,000 lives cut short prematurely because David sinned against God. 70,000 lives that didn't need to be lost, but were because of a poor choice.

You may think that your sin only affects you, and you face the consequences alone, but sometimes, it's not the case. Your choices could cause another's death, or your own, which causes sorrow for those around you. You may think this is an extreme case, but what happens when you make fun of someone every day, and they end up committing suicide because of their low self-esteem. You did the wrong, and someone else suffers for it. You didn't mean for it to happen, but it was a result of your sin.

Every choice has consequences. If you choose sin, don't say you weren't warned. But if you choose Christ, and what's right, you'll never have to worry about what those consequences might be.

Questions

1. Have you ever sinned in such a way where someone else was hurt by it?

_____

_____

_____

_____

2. Have you ever had the consequences of your actions effect those around you?

_____

_____

_____

_____

3. What would you choose out of the choices David had: 3 days of disease, 3 months of being routed by enemies, or 3 years of famine?

    _____

    _____

    _____

    _____

4. Do you think it is fair that others are hurt by your actions? Does this give you a whole different respect for God, who is hurt by all sin, yet was willing to sacrifice His Son for you?

    _____

    _____

    _____

    _____

Man Up Challenge

Every single one of your choices has consequences. You cannot make a single choice that is placed outside of this rule. I want to challenge you to be something different. I want you to be there for someone who is suffering the consequences for their actions. Whether it is a friend who is in the hospital after an accident, a brother or sister who is grounded for the weekend, or a friend of yours who is spending hard time in jail. Be there for someone who is suffering. Share in their suffering as Jesus was there for you in yours.

Day 28: Don't Know the Time

Verses to Read: Matthew 24:36-44

Do you ever watch something and you know what is going to happen? It happens all the time in sports. You watch a game and you see that player, who just had that look, that confidence, that swagger, go up for the ball and haul in the game winning catch when...wait a sec...did I see the ball bounce off his head and roll away? Or how about when there's 1.2 seconds left on the clock and your team's star player goes up for a game winning three and it's nothing...but...rim?

What does this prove? We don't know anything. It's as simple as that. We think we know what's going to happen. We think we know what the "signs" around us are trying to tell us. We think we know that everything in life can be broken down to some simple scientific equation, but whenever we get to that point, it's when you hear the crowd belt out "AIR-BALL!!!!" when the visiting team's player whiffed on that final shot he usually never misses.

Think about the last few years in the NCAA Basketball tournament. Experts and knowledgeable sports guys study months and months and months to come up with the perfect bracket and never get it right. In 2011 alone, out of 2 millions brackets submitted on ESPN.com, only 2 were able to pick the complete Final Four correctly.

We don't know anything when it comes to Christ coming back either. We think we know when it's going to happen. But no one knows that time but God himself. So because of this, we need to be thinking about the actions and the choices we make. Jesus can come back at any second. Even as I'm typing this out, He could come. So the question you need to ask yourself is what do you want to be doing when Jesus comes back? Do you want to be the one with their "hand in the cookie jar" with all the sin you could choose to do, or do you want to be chasing after Him? It may seem like such an easy choice, but when temptation is all around you, it's a choice you need to make every second of every day. So if Jesus was coming back 2 minutes after reading this, what would you want Him to see you doing?

I heard a story of a married man who died at the very young age of 33 years old. It was a sad moment for the family. But it was even worse because of how he died. He died of a heart attack, in his sleep, in the bed of his girlfriend. He had an affair and died while still in his girlfriend's bed. That was his time, and if he had to go face God at that moment, what would he say to explain, as a Christian man who believed in Jesus, why he was in the midst of this affair? Where do you really want to be when God comes back – doing what He asks of you, or doing what you would be ashamed of if you were caught?

Questions

1. Name a time when you thought something was going to happen and you were duped?

   _____

   _____

   _____

   _____

2. Do you think you really know everything? Do you think you know better than God sometimes?

   _____

   _____

   _____

3. Have you ever been busted in sin – caught red handed?

   _____

   _____

   _____

   _____

4. What would be your explanation to God if you were caught in the situation of dying in the midst of an affair?

   _____

   _____

   _____

   _____

Man Up Challenge

Check your life. Check your actions. Check who you are. We all have little things that we do that we think are no big deal. But sin is sin, and we have to see it as exactly that. We shouldn't excuse it in our lives. We do not know when God is coming back, whether it is 5 minutes from now, 5 years or 5 centuries. Let's act if He is coming back any minute, so we live our lives honoring and pleasing Him.

Day 29: Unlimited Power

Verses to Read: Isaiah 40:28-31

This is a verse that always speaks to me when I am sick at home. Have you ever had a time when you came home from work or a game or school or an activity and your body just gave out? I know I have. As much as you try to fight it, as much as you try to get back on your feet as fast as possible, the best thing for you is to just allow yourself to rest and to regain your strength.

But what I do know is that even though I am still relatively young, it doesn't mean I can go forever. I don't have the strength to keep myself running at a high level day after day without allowing myself time to rest. You can still get worn out. The Energizer Bunny's batteries still need replacing at some point – despite what the commercial tries to tell you. It just can't run forever.

There are some of us out there that think we can do everything. If there is a need out there that doesn't have someone answering it, you automatically claim it as yours. Even if it's just a bunch of little things, instead of passing off responsibilities, we are trying instead to do it all ourselves. In some cases, it's a different problem. Instead of doing a few things, we want to do more than we can handle, maximizing every second to be running around doing everything so we feel like we're not missing out. Whichever it is, we do have limits. There is a point where we need time to recharge and not burn out completely.

That's where verse 31 comes in. Our recharge comes from our time with the Lord. How many of us have just been so busy that our time with God gets thrown out? Or how about being so tired that you rather go to bed early than to spend some time in the Word?

It is a common thing; we volunteer to help out with so many activities for the Lord that we think we are spending time with Him by fulfilling our duties. But if our duties get to the point where they distract us from our relationship with God that is when it becomes a problem that needs to be addressed.

If you want to recharge yourself, if you want to get that second wind, if you want to recharge those batteries you've been running on, you need to take time and stop with the Lord. If it's not hard for you to find time to do everything else that you *want* to do in life, why is it so hard to find time to do what you *need* to do?

God will supply the strength, you just need to put your trust in Him, and find time to rest with Him. Don't just replace the batteries, but find the One who has the unlimited power to help you.

Questions

1. Do you run yourself ragged trying to accomplish so many different things with your life?

_____

_____

_____

_____

2. Are there things that you are doing you don't feel called to do, but you're doing it because there is a need?

_____

_____

_____

_____

3. Do you sacrifice your quiet time with God to be able to accomplish more tasks in your life?

_____

_____

_____

_____

4. Why do you think it is so important to just rest and allow your batteries to be recharged?

_____

_____

_____

_____

Man Up Challenge

Make a list of all the activities you are doing – whether they are things you are doing for your family, for your job, for the Lord, or for yourself. Figure out a time when you can stop and recharge your batteries. If you have a family of your own, be the spiritual leader you are meant to be and make it a family time together. Spend time digging into God's Word, reading the Bible as a family and discussing it each night. Don't let your batteries run out. You can't accomplish anything if you don't have the power to do it. Make sure you always stay plugged in to the unlimited power source of our God.

Day 30: Me before God

Verses to Read: Haggai 1:7-11

This is probably a verse most people have never read. Why? Because it's in one of the verses from the minor prophets. And for some reason, these verses are usually the last we want to read, because they're harder to understand. But I think this one is simple. God wants us to give careful thought to our ways. We need to evaluate what we are doing with our lives, and see if it matches up to God's will and what He desires from us.

But doesn't this verse illustrate exactly what we do? We focus on what we want or we need to do first, rather than what God wants. Look at the people in these verses. They lost a war and were thrown into exile for years. Then they come back to their land, and what is the first thing they do? They rebuild their houses and cities. They make sure they have a place to call home and a roof over their own heads. Once they rebuilt their houses, what was next on their list? They started growing food. They need to eat of course, and they need energy to keep going, so the food had to be the next thing on this list. God just sat by waiting, trying to get their attention through making their work return less than expected. But instead of turning to Him for help, they just worked harder, and tried their best to obtain more through their own personal efforts, still not getting their fill when they ate or drank.

Why did this happen? Because they forgot the Lord. The thing that got them into the mess in the first place and sent them far away from the land God promised was how they started living again after God rescues them. Sure, the Lord brought them back and they were happy, but they weren't worshipping in they way He desired to be worshipped. His temple – his house – still stood in ruins. They didn't even try to do anything to fix it, rebuild it, or get it ready to continue offering sacrifices on the altar. It just sat there...ruined, stripped of all its gold, and burnt down. Not only that, they forgot to offer any sacrifices to Him. If there was no temple there was no place to bring their offerings.

So as you focus on your own life today, I have to ask, what are you doing with it? Are you focusing on your own home, your own fields, your own needs, your own desires? Or are you focusing on what God wants of you to focus on, rebuilding His temple, making your faith stronger, thanking Him for how He just rescued you.

Look, it's harder to do the latter, but if you put God first, won't He supply you everything you need, so that the former is taken care of? It's all about priorities. So think today on who gets top billing in your own life.

Questions

1. Do you plan out your days? Does God get a portion of each day or just the leftovers when you have extra time?

_____

_____

_____

_____

2. When God saves you from a situation, do you turn around and continually praise Him, or do you forget about what He just did until you are in the next crisis?

_____

_____

_____

_____

3. Do you leave your faith in ruins until you build up everything that you desire first?

_____

_____

_____

_____

4. Are your priorities upside down and need to be rearranged?

_____

_____

_____

_____

Man Up Challenge

For one week, outside of your regular committed activities (i.e. your job, school, homework, etc.) sacrifice everything else for the Lord. Just allow yourself to stop and focus on God - rebuilding your relationship with Him, spending time with Him, putting Him first in your life. It's easy to say you spend time with God; it is completely different when you sacrifice it all so that He can be the only priority for a period of time. Take the time out and see how it goes. You might be able to see all the little ways you waste time, or neglect God because of these little unnecessary things.

Day 31: Private & Public

Verses to Read: Luke 12:1-3

Why is it that people like their secrets? Why is it that we can't be open about everything that happens in our lives? Because things like shame and guilt are in the world. The whole idea that you're not perfect and that there are flaws in your life need to be hidden and can't be known to the world. Otherwise people might actually realize that you are susceptible to making mistakes.

We all have our secrets, or in some cases, skeletons in our closets. The things we did that we're not proud of, and in most cases we do our best not to slip up and let anyone know there are any skeletons at all. But instead we put on this front that everything is perfect, and we're good Christians, and we don't do anything wrong because that's what good Christians do.

But that's not life. That's not reality. That's not the way it is. We're all broken people. We've all been hurt. We've all been affected by sin. We try to make a public bubble and a private bubble, and as long as what we do in the private bubble doesn't move over to the public one, everything is perfect. We can make our mistakes, commit our sin, hide the truth, and no one would be the wiser about it.

But God knows all. He knows what's in both your public life and your private life. You may not realize it, but like this verse is saying, if your private life is full of some shady and sinful things, it won't take long until it's made known to all. God knows all and will reveal all. If you don't believe me, check the news. Roger Clemens thought his steroid dealings would never be known about. Michael Jackson just passed away and his drug problem which led to his death has come out. Ted Haggard, a well known pastor of a megachurch, thought he was safe with his secret life of drugs and affairs, but that also came out, ruining his personal ministry. Even in the Bible, David thought he got away with committing adultery with Bathsheba, but God exposed that sin as well.

The truth comes out eventually. So this is a call to all Christians with private sin in their lives. You know exactly what that sin is. It's been eating at you for the last so many years. Struggling and struggling and struggling with it, but never yet able to overcome it, or care to because who is ever going to find out?

People with this hidden sin walk the Christian walk in public, but behind closed doors, they're someone who wouldn't resemble one. Choose your master. Let God rule. But if you want to let God rule, let Him rule both your public and private lives; you can't just choose one or the other.

Questions

1. Do you have sin in your life you are afraid to let others know about?

_____

_____

_____

_____

2. Are you still struggling with this sin? Is it effecting your relationship with God?

_____

_____

_____

_____

3. Why are you still struggling? Do you want to give up this sin? Are you happy doing what you're doing?

_____

_____

_____

_____

4. Do you try to live 2 lives – a public and private one?

_____

_____

_____

_____

5. Do you think you are the exception that will never be found out?

_____

_____

_____

_____

Man Up Challenge

It's time to make your private and public lives match up with one another. I know you don't even have to think for more than 5 seconds to know what you are struggling with. It's a foothold Satan has in your life. Admit your mistake to a friend you can confide in, your pastor, or someone who will go through the struggle with you. Ask them to pray and continually check up on you about it. It is a humbling experience, but the only way to overcome the sin is to have people set up who will challenge you to be pure.

Day 32: Pointing Out Flaws

Verses to Read: Matthew 7:1-5

Are you the type of person who always likes to pick apart the mistakes of others? You're super critical of the choices they make and want to drop them down a notch by showing how you know better?

Well, this verse is a very important one. It tells us God will judge us the way we judge others. Think about that for a second. How would you feel if God judged you the same way you judge the person who hurt you? How would you be judged if God judged you the same way you judged that person in your class or on the job who got caught drinking? How would you be judged if God judged you the same way for your sin as you judged someone else for theirs?

We have to remember that sin is sin and we all have it. There's no such thing as a lesser sin. A white lie equals murder. It's not just a lesser crime. So the next time we go out into the world, let us remember that it's not our place to judge others for their actions, it's our job to love people. Some people's sin is more visible than others as well, and just because they are more apparent, doesn't make them cause for more scrutiny than those who sin in private. We don't like our sin being pointed out and to be made to feel less than a person for what we do wrong, so let's not do it to others. If we do, it's the way we will be judged by our Lord and Savior Jesus Christ. Billy Graham said it best, "It's the Spirit's job to convict. It's God's job to judge. It's my job to love."

I already stated this, but I want to ask it anyways: How many of you have sin in your life? The answer to this is pretty obvious...and most would probably shoot off Romans 3:23 the second they read it. Now the second question is a little different but sounds the same. How many of you are still struggling with sin in your life?

This verse speaks of people who want to fix the sin of others, while ignoring the sin in their own life. It talks about people who want to help people take out the minor sin in their lives, while not realizing they have a much bigger problem on their hands.

We need to start being concerned with the sin in our lives. Some people may have overcome some or most of the issues with sin in their lives, but still struggle with others. But being "perfect" or "almost perfect" in our own walks doesn't give us the right to be insulting, degrading, or putting down other Christians who are still struggling. Truth is, if you have the mindset that you're almost perfect, you might be building up a pride issue. Worry about strengthening your relationship with God first.

As for others, we need to be helping each other through prayer and accountability, and not pointing out people's faults. As I said before, you don't like people pointing out your sin, why do it to someone else? It's our job to love people; let's show them what true love is all about.

Questions

1. Have you ever compared yourself to another Christian to make yourself feel better about your actions?

   _____

   _____

   _____

   _____

2. Have you ever justified your sin as being "not so bad" because of what others do?

   _____

   _____

_____

_____

3. Have you ever called someone out for their sin, while having your own sin fester?

_____

_____

_____

_____

4. Do you think you are "perfect" or "almost perfect" with your walk with the Lord?

_____

_____

_____

_____

Man Up Challenge

It's time to take an assessment of your own life. Look deep into the cracks and ask God to reveal the sin of your life. Many of us think we have everything under control, but the truth is, sin is always hiding where we least suspect it. Let's take these verses to heart and inspect ourselves to find that log in our own eyes, before trying to take the speck out of others.

Day 33: Whitewashed Tombs

Verses to Read: Matthew 23:27-28

I read this verse and I have to say I was very convicted by it. Jesus said this about the Pharisees. These guys were like the self-appointed and recognized leaders of the synagogue. These guys were the ones who had all the answers when someone had a question about the Jewish faith.

But look at what Jesus said to them. He called them hypocrites. He said they may look clean and perfect on the outside, but they are wasting away on the inside. What does this translate to? Jesus was saying that they were looking perfect on the outside: they present themselves well with their nice clothes and perfect hygiene, they always had that cheesy fake smile on, and never seemed to have a problem in the world, never sinned, and always knew the right answer.

But at the same time, on the inside, where their heart was, it was nothing but dead bones: they told people to do one thing, yet did the opposite themselves.

They lied, they cheated, they stole, and they ended up having a life completely different from the front you see.

And then I look at my own life, and I realize all the mistakes I have made in the past, and all the mistakes I still make. The past is the past, and there's nothing we can do about it, except to ask God for forgiveness and learn from it. But what's going on right now, the sin that's festering in our lives, we need to take care of it. We need to put an end to it. We need to find a way to clear it out.

The truth is, the one thing people can see most is if someone is faking. If you're saying you're a jock. but you don't play any sports, you're going to be called a liar. If you're saying you're a Christian, and you're not living the Christian life, you're going to be called a liar too. Saying you're a Christian and not living the lifestyle can't be done. I know most want to take pieces of Christianity, and live as the world lives, but the truth is, all you're being is a hypocrite. Showing up to church on Sunday with all the answers, and then forgetting about God until next Sunday, is being a hypocrite. Praising God with all your heart through song, only to use that same voice to swear at someone who offended you, is being a hypocrite.

Christianity isn't something you can just put on and take off when you want. It isn't a "Sunday" thing or an "only when you're in church" thing, it's an "all aspects of your life" thing. My prayer for you today is to see if you are who you say you are. If you say you're a Christian, are you living it? Is it part of who you are when you're in school, playing sports, hanging with your friends? Or is it only when it's convenient for you? Don't be a Pharisee. Don't be a hypocrite. Let God take the place as Lord of your life and let Him be a part of both the inside and out.

Questions

1. Let's get to the heart of the issue – why are you reading this book? Why do you go to church every Sunday? Why are you a Christian?

   _____

   _____

   _____

   _____

2. Is this Christianity you ascribe to something you follow daily or only when it is convenient?

    _____

    _____

    _____

    _____

3. What are you doing right now that is hypocritical to the faith you say you believe in? We all have something. If you write down nothing, you're not looking hard enough.

    _____

    _____

    _____

    _____

4. Can you honestly say your faith has changed your life – not just what you do – but your heart?

    _____

    _____

    _____

    _____

Man Up Challenge

It's time to get real. It's time to step up and be a man. We don't need any more poser, fake wannabe Christians out there who tell everyone they have it all together when they don't. It's time to do a manly thing and get vulnerable. The next time you are in church, be real. Be who you are. Let people know you're struggling, or hurting, or if you have a need, or you don't have everything together. If you can't do this in the one place where it's okay to be who you are, then all you're doing is not being yourself, not being real, and just being another faker in the crowd.

Day 34: Questioning God

Verses to Read: Habakkuk 1:1-2:1

Now I have to say this is one of the gutsiest verses of the Bible. Why? Because He's challenging God. The prophet Habakkuk asked God a question, "Why do those who sin in Israel have their sin go unpunished?" And God replies by saying, "I'm going to deal with them by sending the Babylonians to destroy them." So Habakkuk listens to God's response, and says, "Hold the phone, you're doing to do what?!?! Send even worse people to destroy us? How is that right?" And then he pretty much tells God He has a lot of explaining to do, and He's going to wait for his answer, because it's going to be a "good" one. To me, I wonder why God didn't strike Him down with fire for talking to Him the way he did.

But then I got to thinking, how many times have I done that to God? "God, why didn't you give me the skills to throw a 95 mph fastball?" "God, why did you have to take my best friend away at such a young age?"

"God, why do you let bad things happen to good people, and good things happen to bad people?" I think I could fill up the rest of this book with questions, but you get the point. We question God. We question His motives. We question His plan. We question if He really has our best interests in mind. We question if He really cares at all for us, or if something happened while He "wasn't looking." We even question His ability to act.

But God does have a plan and everything happens for His good purpose. Yeah, bad things happened. Bad things will always happen. You can blame God for it, but it's not His fault. He made the world perfect, and we screwed it up. We brought the sin into the world. We said to Him that He was holding back from us, and we did what we wanted. Sin destroys relationships. It ruined our relationship with God, each other, the earth, the animals, everything and everyone. We destroy them all, and we're blaming God for our own action.

Bad things happen. They happen every day, and unfortunately, they will continue to happen. But even though we only see it from a small perspective – from our pain, frustration, anger, sorrow - doesn't mean good won't come out of it. God is in control. God is in charge. Sometimes we will see the good of the mess we're in. Other times, we won't. But whether we do or don't isn't the issue. We need to honor and worship our God with all our heart. His plan is perfect, even if for a moment, we just don't realize it.

Some people, as I have seen on the news, will question God asking, "Is God distant and won't help or there and unloving? He is neither. He is a present, active, loving God. We cannot blame God for our actions. We made this mess and we must live with it, instead of using God as a scapegoat.

Questions

1. Do you ever question God about what happens in this world?

   _____

   _____

   _____

   _____

2. Do you ever question God about why He didn't make you different?

   _____

   _____

_____

_____

3. Do you ever blame God for all the bad things that happen in the world that He doesn't stop? Why do you think it is His fault?

_____

_____

_____

_____

Man Up Challenge

God wants to know how we feel about things, but yet at times we feel like we can't approach God and question what happens. But it is time to be bold about it. During your prayer time, just have a conversation with Him. Let Him know all of your fears, frustrations, and questions about why things have been going the way they've been going. You may be surprised to know that even though He knows your every thought, just by asking Him might get you the answer you have been looking for.

Day 35: Garbage In, Garbage Out

Verses to Read: Luke 6:43-45

What type of fruit have you been producing lately? It's a tough question to answer. It's always a tough question to answer when it has something to do with evaluating your life and the choices that you make on a daily basis. So are you one who is producing good fruit or bad fruit?

If you're one producing good fruit, you truly understand your faith. You're running after God, doing what you need to do to follow Him. You do it out of your great love for Him. You understand what Jesus suffered on the cross and want to act out that love by being a living sacrifice for others. People see your actions, and everything you do and realize your actions show what you believe.

If you're one producing bad fruit, you're not one who grasps the whole concept of following Jesus. Living a life for Jesus is to live a life of repentance. To repent literally means "to turn from." To turn from the sin, to turn from our desires, to turn from the evil impulses in our life and to turn to Jesus. Maybe there is sin in your life that you just haven't been able to overcome and it's stopping you from chasing after Jesus 100%. Maybe you just don't want to get rid of it because you don't want to follow Jesus 100%. Maybe 10, 20 or 30% is good enough for you. Maybe you just want to keep living that old life, and like the way things were, rather than changing into what is best for your faith. Whatever it may be, it's stopping you from producing anything but bad, rotten fruit.

I know you probably have heard of the expression, whatever you put into your heart, that's what you're going to give in return. If you listen to music with swears, your mouth will probably produce words you shouldn't be saying. If you put in pornography, you're going to produce lust and an unhealthy view of women and relationships. If you put in lies, it's probably all you're going to say, and you will be known as a person who should not be trusted. If you put in violence, you're probably going to lash out and think it is an okay and healthy practice. It's the "garbage in, garbage out" mentality.

So check out what you're producing. If there's something that's ruining your fruit, check to see if it's something you need to fix, otherwise you'll be wasting a perfectly good crop.

Questions

1. What type of fruit have you been producing in your life?

_____

_____

_____

_____

2. Do you live your life in "repentance mode" – in such a way that you have turned from everything else, considering it all nothing, to follow after Jesus?

_____

_____

_____

_____

3. Do you think offering only a portion of yourself to God is good enough?

_____

_____

_____

_____

4. Does the "garbage in, garbage out" model makes sense to you? Do you believe it? Do you think this is how it works?

_____

_____

_____

_____

Man Up Challenge

It's time for more self-reflection. What type of fruit are you producing? Are you putting in things like lies, violence, pornography, improper music into your thought process and expecting to not produce the same fruit in your life? Look it is garbage in, and garbage out. So it's time to take out the trash. If you are placing garbage into your head, it is time to remove it from your lifestyle. Jesus doesn't fit into your lifestyle, you transform your life to fit with His. It's a huge difference. So look at what doesn't fit and start filling the garbage bags.

Day 36: Tough Questions

Verses to Read: Luke 14:25-35

Some people look at these verses and get a completely wrong impression of what they have to say. Some will argue that Jesus was against loving your own family, or Jesus was a man who believed in hating others. Both of these statements are very untrue. What Jesus was doing was letting people know of what type of cost or commitment it will take to follow Him, and to see if they were ready to make it.

He was letting people think about these tough questions. What would you do if I asked you to follow me, and your father or mother tried to stop you? What if your parents said they would disown you for following me, would you still do it? Would you still be willing to follow me then? If that doesn't bother you, what if it was your wife and children? What if your wife told you that if you get baptized she will take your child and run away, and you will never see either of them again, would you still go under the water? What if my Father called you to serve in a remote village in Africa and they were totally and in most cases, violently against hearing what you have to say, would you still be willing to go? Then Jesus goes even deeper...what if I ask you to lay it all down - everything you love...everything you know...everything that means the most to you...even your life for me...what would be your answer? Can I count on you to give me your own life if it means that others will get to know who I am?

These are tough questions. Questions that could rack your brain for days, months or even years. But what Jesus was getting at was serving Him requires devotion. It requires priority. Your family, your friends, your livelihood, you career, your life - what are these things to you? For most people, these would be the most important things in your life, the things you treasure most. The things you would never want to give up under any circumstances.

What Jesus was saying in these verses was - am I even on this most treasured list? Am I one of these things you are unwilling to give up? He deserves to be the #1 person on that list, but is He even on it at all? Is something we're doing dragging us away from what He desires of us?

Hate is a strong word, and Jesus would not condone hating anyone, because our God is a God of love. But when we're looking at the cost of following Jesus, are you willing to sacrifice it all, pick up that cross and walk, knowing the things that matter most to you may be left behind in the process?

Questions

1. How much would you be willing to give up for Jesus? Your family? Your parents? Your wife? Your children? Your best friends? Your career? Your life? Would there be anything you would say is way too much or impossible for you to let go?

   _____

   _____

   _____

   _____

2. What does the word devotion mean to you? Do you think you have the same devotion to Jesus as you have to whatever matters most in your life?

   _____

   _____

_____

_____

3. Is Jesus one of the people/items on your most
    treasured list?

    _____

    _____

    _____

    _____

4. Are you willing to sacrifice it all for Jesus?

    _____

    _____

    _____

    _____

Man Up Challenge

Saying it and doing it are not the same thing. You could
write whatever you want under the questions above, try
to impress who ever picks up this book and reads it after
you with your best Sunday School answers possible, but
the only thing that impresses is action. Live you life for

the next week as if Jesus was your #1 priority. It's something that should be that way for your whole life in the first place, but I am giving you a one-week challenge. Then think about how different your life was than normal. I bet if you honestly took this challenge seriously, you would never want to put your life back to the way it used to be.

Day 37: The Next Big Thing

Verses to Read: Ecclesiastes 2:1-11

Have you ever wanted something really bad? It could be the newest gaming system, the newest iPad, the newest phone, the fastest, slickest car, even the biggest HD 3D TV money can buy. Whatever it is, is there something inside you that just overwhelms you and make you think, "I must have it!"?

So what do you do? Do everything in your power to possess it. If you're young enough, you first ask your parents, and I would say 90% of the time after they laugh in your face, you get a job. So like most of us who work and want to get something, you struggle and toil and work for the next so many months of your life to earn and save enough cash to buy this special "toy" of yours. And when you finally earn enough money to get it, how does it make you feel? Great...but only for a little while. After a few months, you might still be enjoying the fruits of your labor, but it doesn't have the same charm it once did. You realize that you're missing something else...or even worse yet, a newer, better version of what you wanted has come out. So what happens? You start the cycle all over again. And it just keeps going on and on forever – never being satisfied, never being fulfilled.

In this passage, Solomon, who wrote this book, is king of Israel. He's living the good life. Arguably the best life of anyone who has ever lived in their given time. He has pretty much everything. He had numerous wives and concubines. He has tons of gold and riches. All the countries around him respected him and feared him. It was said that the gold in the temple Solomon built for the Lord contained $2 Billion worth of gold by today's standards. And He had his own treasure on top of that. It's easy to say that money was no object to this guy. And also as king, he had power. He could do anything he wanted, and just throw his money around to get his way. He spoke the people listened.

And then you just hear his words in these verses. He let himself have everything he desired. He didn't hold himself back from anything...and it was all meaningless. He called it chasing after the wind. Something that is just so impossible to do, because even if you did run as fast as the wind, how were you going to contain it? Running after stuff is meaningless. It's pointless. No matter how hard you try to fill that void you have with material objects, it'll never be enough. There's only one that can fill that void, and it's Jesus. He's the one who's meant to be there, and the only one that can make you whole again.

Questions

1. What is an item you wanted so bad you would do anything to get it? How did it make you feel when you finally got it? How long did it take before you didn't really care about it anymore, or wanted to get the updated model?

   _____

   _____

   _____

   _____

2. Do you believe you can get something new, and have it fill the void in your life once and for all to bring you happiness?

   _____

   _____

   _____

3. If you are saving up money right now for a specific item, what could you do with that money instead to serve someone else?

    _____

    _____

    _____

    _____

Man Up Challenge

I bet some of you know what I am going to challenge you with before reading this. Take your answer for question number 3 and do it. Instead of purchasing something for yourself which will only bring you joy for a temporary amount of time, purchase something for someone else who is in need. Look, you can get something for yourself, but what will you gain? Nothing. So why not give it to someone else instead, and bring a little happiness to someone who needs it right now.

Days 38: Raise Them High!

Verses to Read: Exodus 17:8-16

How many of you are tired? How many of you just feel completely worn out? As I write this, I am feeling this way. It is about 12 midnight and I still have so much to do, but I feel like I could sleep for the next week. But at the same time, I have stuff that needs to get done sooner rather than later. I have been asked by God to commit myself to Him and to do His work, even if it means I have to sacrifice some of my rest to do it.

That is what happened here with Moses. Moses had a job to do. Moses needed to make sure the Israelites kept fighting hard and won their battle. To do that, Moses had to keep his hands up for hours. As long as his hands stayed raised, the Israelites would win the battle, but if he ever lowered them, they would be defeated. It's a tough job. I don't know if you ever had to keep your arms up for a long period of time, but it's not an easy thing to do. It sounds like one of the challenges you would find on Survivor to receive immunity.

And over time, Moses got tired. Moses was worn out. Moses lost strength. And Moses' arms, started to fall very slowly. And the Israelites started to lose the battle. But that didn't mean it was over. Aaron and Hur didn't just let the Israelites die and be slaughtered by the Amalekites, and didn't allow Moses to get tired. They did what needed to be done. They came alongside Moses. They gave him a rock to sit on, and the used their own strength to help him keep his arms up for the rest of the day. What an amazing picture of help when someone is weak.

Well the same goes for us. What Aaron and Hur did for Moses, Jesus did for us. He gave us His Spirit. Jesus gave us the one thing to give us the strength and power we need to do everything He desires of us. So the next time you feel tired, and you can't go on, just remember God is there holding up your arms, even when you feel like they can't stay up anymore. We're not alone. We never will be. Jesus will be there every step of the way. Trust in the Lord and ask Him for strength, and you'll be amazed at what He will give you. Even if you just want to be in bed.

We also need to return the favor that God has done for us by doing it for others around us – just as Aaron and Hur did for Moses. We need to be there for people who are tired and weary. We probably know a lot of people who are overworked, stressed, and tired, yet they have no one to rely on to help them during their time of need. So step up and be that person. Don't let their exhaustion get the best of them.

Questions

1. Have you ever been so tired that you couldn't even get up out of bed or off the couch? What did you need to do to finish what had to be done?

_____

_____

_____

_____

2. Had you ever had an experience that your actions would single-handedly determine the results of an event, like what Moses went through?

_____

_____

_____

_____

3. Do you have friends who will come along side you when you are overworked and overtired?

_____

_____

_____

_____

4. Have you ever been there for someone who was overburdened? How did it make you feel to help them out?

_____

_____

_____

_____

Man Up Challenge

Your job is to go out and help take a burden off someone. We all know people who are tired, who are word out, who go above and beyond the call of duty on a daily basis, so now is the time to allow them to take a rest and for you to help them. Whether it is to help them with a task on their to do list, or to just be willing to take them out to dinner and give them a break – do something to let them know they are not alone – just as Jesus is always there for us when we think we are.

Day 39: Golden Rule

Verses to Read: Matthew 7:9-12

This verse is the golden rule. A rule that is known in Christianity to be important, but pretty much every major religion also has a saying like it as well. But the question I have is how well do we follow it, and how do we react when others don't?

Usually this is the scenario. You're hanging out with friends and you get a phone call from another, asking for you to help him or her out. They're volunteering at a road race tomorrow morning at 8am passing out water to tired runners as they go by. You decide although you should be there, you really need your sleep because after all, you're staying out late with your friends. If he or she called you a few days before, gave you at least a little more notice, you would probably be more willing to go, but since they're last minute, forget it. You'd rather be having fun and getting your sleep.

Fast forward a few weeks, when you have a need. You were put in charge of an event that needs about eight volunteers and one backed out leaving a hole you need to fill ASAP. So you call around to those you think could help, even your friend who needed your help a few weeks earlier, and they decline. How do you feel at this point? You're mad, upset, and think they're being selfish only thinking about themselves.

And here we are. We're Christians. We're called to serve those in need. We're called to be the example to sacrifice like Jesus sacrificed for us. So when we see people in need, are we the first ones to step up and say yes? More often than not, we are the ones who bury our heads or try not to make eye contact. We're more likely the ones to try to think of another person to ask. We're more likely to be the one who begrudgingly places up their hand half-heartedly because no one else would, and yet we're the ones who get mad when others do it back to us. It can't work both ways.

We as Christians are called to love. To love is to sacrifice – just as Jesus Christ showed His love for us by laying down His life. We need to be sacrificing our time and energy for the ones who matter to us. Truth is, if a friend is in dire straits and needs help, and you don't go running, are you really loving them the way Christ would? Whatever the need, whatever the sacrifice, whatever the hurt, we need to love and serve those around us. If all of us as Christians would just be willing to help when there's a need, instead of only focusing on our own, think about all the amazing things we can accomplish for the glory of our God!

Questions

1. When have you ever had a need and no one was willing to help you out? What were you feeling at the time?

_____

_____

_____

_____

2. When is the last time you answered the call for help from someone else?

_____

_____

_____

_____

3. What usually stops you from volunteering when someone has a need?

_____

_____

_____

_____

4. What can you do to be more willing to sacrifice?

_____

_____

_____

_____

Man Up Challenge

This might take a ton of courage but you're going to have to be a man and do it. The next time you are at church, or at a meeting, or at a function, and someone asks for help – be the first one to volunteer to help out. Don't wait to see if anyone else will step up, don't put your hand up in disgust, don't try to pawn the job off on someone else. You volunteer, help out, and follow through. The more you're willing to help out and step out in faith, the easier it will be to continue serving.

Day 40: Nothing Can Separate

Verses to Read: Romans 8:31-38

Think about these verses for a second. What a passage of hope. What a passage of peace. What a passage about the true love of our God.

This list encompasses everything. No power will ever be strong enough, no distance will ever be far enough, and not even death would even have the ability to pull us away from our Lord. God's love has always been and will also be greater, and that is something that cannot be taken away from us.

This is even true when you're at your lowest, and you feel so far away from God. You've been walking away from Him. Not reading your Bible, not praying, not giving Him any time at all. You're in the middle of your own spiritual rut. A place where God is not present anymore because you neglected Him and forged your path through the forest in a different direction.

And on top of that, you turned to sin during this time, and might even have done something you think would be unforgivable - something God would never be able to forgive under any circumstances. You're in your lowest possible pit. You're unreachable. You're unattainable. You're unforgiveable. You're unlovable.

But no matter how far you may think you've moved away from Him, no matter how bad you may have been, no matter if you think the sin you've racked up in your life is too great, God is always within reach. You may think you're 99 feet away, but God's arms can reach 100. He has His arms out, reaching for you, and all you have to do, the one thing you need to do to accept His love, is to reach back.

God's love for you is something that cannot be fully measured, cannot be fully explained, and cannot be fully comprehended. When we think of love, we think of a give and take relationship. We think that we need to do something for God so that God can love us. But God doesn't work in this way. God's love is deeper – it is a self-sacrificial love – an agape love.

The word agape in Greek that we translate as love – means that God will do anything to let you know how much He loves you. In reality, it meant sacrificing His own Son on a cross. If you're a father, could you imagine doing something so radical – even for someone you loved with all your heart? But what makes it even more bizarre, is that He did it for people who did not love Him back. He did for those who did nothing to deserve this gift.

And so, if God can take a sinner like me, or a sinner like Paul, who wrote this passage – a man with the blood of Christians on his hands, and still love and accept us despite how much we shoved Him away, despite how many times we said, "I don't need you," to His face, and despite how much we willingly sin against Him, then like Paul, I'm persuaded too that God's love will always prevail, and will always bring us back to Him.

Questions

1. Have you done something in your life that you consider unforgivable? What was it?

_____

_____

_____

_____

2. Before picking up this book, were you in a dry spell in your faith life? What was it lacking? What was missing?

_____

_____

_____

_____

3. What is the biggest sacrifice you would make for someone you love?

_____

_____

_____

_____

4. What would be the biggest sacrifice you'd make for someone you hate?

_____

_____

_____

_____

5. Do you believe God will always love you despite all your past and future mistakes?

_____

_____

_____

_____

Man Up Challenge

Sacrifice something for someone you do not like. The best way to understand what God did for us is to do the same for another. I'm not asking you to sacrifice your children – but step up today and do something for someone you typically wouldn't. It could be to mow their lawn, buy them lunch at work, or just do the tedious paperwork you fight over each day. Man up and step out, and jot down your thoughts afterwards.

Tim Baker

It's Over...or Is It?

Well, you have done it. You have gotten through the whole entire book. I know that this book has probably stretched you, challenged you, and pushed you in ways you didn't even imagine were possible. But praise God, if you took this seriously, you are hopefully enjoying a closer relationship with your Lord and Savior Jesus Christ.

However, I wanted to leave you with one more Man Up Challenge. I ask you to please do not let what you read in this book go to waste. Most Christians go to an event, a retreat, or read a book, and are on a spiritual high when they finish. But a few days later, they are back to their old ways and their old habits as if nothing ever happened.

Do not let this happen to you. Don't backslide. Don't give up. Always push forward and continue to grow. Don't consider finishing these challenges as an end, but the beginning of your new, powerful life in Jesus.

God bless you!

ABOUT THE AUTHOR

Tim Baker is a Suffolk University grad with a B.S. in Biology, and a M. Div from Gordon-Conwell Theological Seminary. Tim labels himself is a "science geek" and a "Jesus freak." After serving churches in Massachusetts and Alaska over the last 10 years, he currently serves as the Associate Minister at Hillside Christian Church in Sinking Spring, PA.

Tim is married to his wife, Amy, who he claims is the most amazing and beautiful girl in the world. They are expecting their first child, Gabriel at the end of 2011.